# The Second Madame: A Memoir of Elizabeth Charlotte, Duchesse D'Orleans

Mary Louise McLaughlin

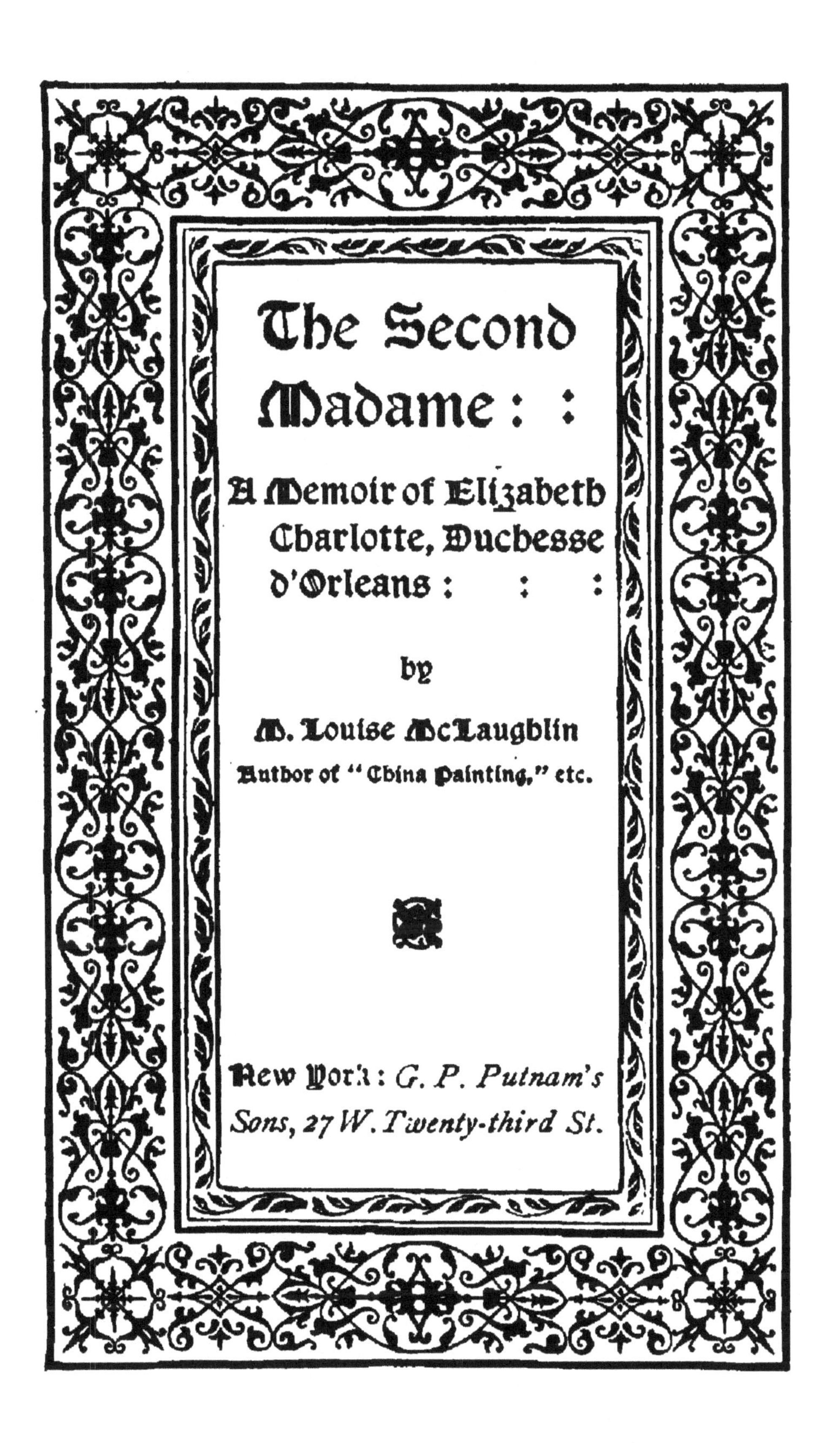

# The Second Madame : :

## A Memoir of Elizabeth Charlotte, Duchesse d'Orleans : : :

by

M. Louise McLaughlin
Author of "China Painting," etc.

New York : *G. P. Putnam's Sons, 27 W. Twenty-third St.*

# HEADPIECES.

CHAPTER PAGE

## CHAPTER I.

### THE LETTERS.

IN November, 1671, Elizabeth Charlotte, daughter of the Elector Palatine, was brought to France to become the second wife of Philippe Duc d'Orleans, or, Monsieur, as he was called; the brother of Louis XIV. The marriage had been arranged for purely political reasons, and the unfortunate young princess was but the unwilling and unheeded instrument in the establishment of friendly relations between two powers. The position thus assumed was a brilliant one, but, apart from that consideration, it seemed a cruel fate which assigned her to this destiny.

The unhappy relations of Monsieur with his first wife, the beautiful Henrietta of England; the suspicious circumstances attending her death; the horrible rumors, which, though proven to be unfounded, had yet the effect of connecting her husband with her sudden taking-off; the contemptible character of the man;—all tended to insure little domestic felicity to the young bride. Monsieur was, simply, what his education had made him—the foil of his stronger brother. His tutors had been instructed not to make a clever man of him, and so well had they followed their instructions that he was, throughout his life, effeminate, vain, and frivolous, the prey of his favorites, and the dupe of all who wished to use him for their own purposes.

The suspicion that Monsieur had had something to do with the untimely death of his first wife was even shared by his brother, the King. St. Simon, who claimed to have heard the story many years afterward, from a very good source, said that, on the night after the death of Henrietta, Louis, who had heard that a member of Monsieur's household could throw some light upon the matter, got up after he had retired, so anxious was he to learn the truth, and sent for the man. He was conveyed to the presence of the King under a strong guard, and questioned as to what he knew. He was promised pardon if he implicated himself, and threatened with instant death if he refused to answer. Thus urged, he revealed the names of the other two men engaged in the plot, one of whom had sent the poison from Italy, while the other had placed it in the drinking-cup of Madame. The King then asked if his brother knew of the plans of the conspirators, and was answered that, as it was well known that Monsieur could not keep a secret, no one had been foolish enough to tell him. Upon receiving this answer, the King drew a deep breath of relief and dismissed the witness.

This man was the chief steward of Monsieur's household. He held the position when the second Madame arrived. A day or so after her arrival, the King had a private interview with her, and told her all about the matter, assuring her that if he had not believed his brother innocent he never would have permitted him to marry her. Madame kept her own counsel, and after a while managed to get rid of the undesirable steward; but it may be imagined that the knowledge of his connection with this affair could not have been a very agreeable introduction to her new life. It is no wonder that she wrote, years afterward: "If my father had had for me as great attachment as I had for him, he would not have sent me into a country as dangerous as this; I came only from obedience, not from choice." Later, when Madame came to have confidential relations with the Dauphine, a Bavarian princess, this companion in misfortune remarked that, while they were both unhappy, she deserved her fate as she had been determined to marry the Dauphin, while Madame had, as she knew, been sent to France against her will.

Long afterward, when there had been ample opportunity of testing the truth of what she said, Madame wrote to her aunt: "I would think grandeur very well if one had everything with it, that is to say, plenty of money to be magnificent, to do good, and to punish; but to have only the name of grandeur without money to supply the necessary wants, and to be strained and to have no society, that is very much against my taste, for, if I confess the truth, I hold that nothing is to be more esteemed than a position in which one can be cheerful with one's friends without the embarrassment of greatness, and can do what one wills with one's own."

According to the terms of Madame's marriage contract, Monsieur had control of her property, and while she brought him a large dowry which he squandered at the gaming table, she complained that she had not the disposal of a farthing. Monsieur cared little for her, and the favorites who had caused the death of his first wife remained to annoy the second.

The young wife found herself an alien in a strange land, and never during her long residence in it did she reconcile herself to its customs. Outspoken to the point of rudeness, proud, very unprepossessing in appearance, she made few friends. Thrown largely on her own resources, she sought distraction in correspondence with friends and relatives left behind in her beloved Fatherland. It is rather a pathetic figure to which we are introduced, alone every evening scribbling sheet after sheet to her confidants. Almost every day a courier departed in one direction or another, carrying these precious missives. One day was devoted to the correspondents in one country, the next to those of another, while Saturday was set apart to the bringing up of all arrears. The magnitude of the work may be judged by the fact that she wrote every day except when incapacitated by illness or the pressure of unusual occupations, and that she frequently wrote forty or fifty pages a day. The correspondence, moreover, extended over a period of fifty years, for, in spite of her many trials, Madame lived to be seventy.

Her letters were chiefly addressed to her aunt, the Electress Sophia; her half-sisters, the Countesses Louise and Amelie Elizabeth; her former governess, Fräulein Von Offeln, afterward Frau Von Harling; her step-daughters, the Queens of Spain and of Sardinia, and, later, to her own daughter, the Duchess of Lorraine. From the contents of these letters, it would hardly be guessed that the writer was aware they were subjected to rigid official oversight. Madame's suspicions on this point were, however, probably only too well founded, as, indeed, upon one occasion, she had positive and very unpleasant demonstration. Usually, this inspection merely caused delay, of which she complained as follows: "I know why my letters come to you irregularly; it is the fault of the director of the post. He wants to read all in order to make extracts that he may show the King if he wishes, and as he does not know any German he must have them translated. I do not like his attentions." But the task of the officials upon whom devolved the overseeing of this correspondence must have been no light one. Madame's handwriting was almost illegible and her language a curious compound of all the tongues of which she had any knowledge. German was, naturally, the usual medium, but many French words were introduced with others which were, apparently, inventions of her own, the whole badly spelled and punctuated in a most original fashion. She was superior to all rules, and her pen flew over the pages, passing from one subject to another without any perceptible transition. Sometimes she arrested the flow of words, with tardy caution, saying, "I know all my letters are opened," or, "There is much one cannot say in a letter." One can but imagine what these letters would have been had they not been opened. As it was, and in spite of the fact that the writer knew the minions of the post might read all she wrote, she exercised the utmost freedom in what she said as well in the manner of saying it. Her expressions were frequently very coarse, revoltingly coarse to modern eyes, untranslatable into modern language. We must remember, however, that this was the manner of the time and that the conversation of the richly dressed ladies and gentlemen of the court of Louis XIV. would have been equally shocking considered in the light of modern standards.

With all due allowance for the prejudices of a foreigner who looked with little favor on the life about her, it is not a pleasant picture that is revealed in Madame's correspondence. She possessed a keen sense of humor, however, which was combined with a freedom from conventionality that led her to express herself with the most refreshing candor. These qualities brightened the realistic and somewhat repulsive portrait. Altogether, this voluminous correspondence furnishes a unique contribution to the literature of the time, and gives a most entertaining picture of its manners and customs. Against the dark background of vice, intrigue, and frivolity, the woman herself stands forth a pure and shining light in that most licentious court. A faithful wife and devoted mother, her virtues seem all the greater by contrast with others in whom these domestic qualities were so conspicuously absent.

The King was always kind to his sister-in-law, and although this conduct might have been expected from so politic a monarch toward one so highly connected as Madame, yet we should, perhaps, give him credit for perceiving the sterling virtues hidden under the brusque exterior of the uncompromising dame. As for her, the great respect for rank which was one of her most distinguishing characteristics led her to regard the King with the almost superstitious veneration she considered due to his position.

A letter written by Madame from St. Germain, December 14, 1676, to her aunt the Electress Sophia, gives an idea of her life at the French court at this time.

"Ever Beloved, I humbly beg your pardon

for having delayed writing such an everlastingly long time. In the first place, at Versailles, there was something to do the whole day. In the morning and until three o'clock in the afternoon we were at the chase. When we came in we dressed and went to play, where they stayed until seven o'clock in the evening; from there they went to the comedy, which was out at half-past ten; then to supper; from supper to the ball, which lasted until three o'clock in the morning; and then to bed. From that you can well imagine that I have had no time to write." Then follows an account of a fall from her horse, while hunting, which had been the cause of many, to her, annoying visits of inquiry. Her horse had started while she was arranging her habit and she had been thrown out of the saddle. She had, however, kept her foot in the stirrup and had watched her opportunity to slip to the ground without injury. The King had manifested the greatest concern, being the first to come to her, pale as death, to inquire if she was hurt, and although she assured him she was not, he had insisted on feeling her head all over to see if it had been injured.

She continued as follows: "The King gives me daily evidences of his favor; he speaks to me everywhere he meets me, and lets me take medianoche with him and Madame de Montespan every Saturday. This makes me very much the fashion, and whatever I do, whether it be good or very much out of the way, excites the admiration of the courtiers to such a degree that when I put on my old sables on account of the cold, to keep my neck warmer, every one took pattern and it is now the highest fashion, which makes me laugh, as these same people, who now admire this fashion and copy it, five years ago, abused my sables so freely and so much that I have not since dared put them on.

"So it goes always in this court, where the courtiers fancy one is in favor one can do what he wishes and be assured that it will be approved, but if they fancy the contrary, he would be held up for ridicule though he came from heaven. Would to God that it might come about that my Ever Beloved could spend a month here and see the life ; I know very well we would often laugh heartily."

Madame was not, however, always in such favor with the people about her. She seems to have taken little pains to remain in their good graces, and she had some enemies who gave her a great deal of trouble. These were the favorites of Monsieur who were always intriguing to do her injury. There is a letter to her aunt, written in September, 1682, in which an account of a difficulty between herself and Monsieur, brought about by his associates, is detailed at great length in German and French. To end the matter, Madame said she begged the King to let her retire to a convent, but he would not consent, telling her that her place was in the court, and he would never allow her to go away. Peace was restored between the ill-mated couple for the time being.

Necessarily these domestic troubles in high life could not be altogether concealed, and in one of her letters Madame complained that she and Monsieur had been watched beyond measure, and that people had said that they lived a cat-and-dog life. In November 24, 1682, she wrote to her aunt: "I can assure you, my Ever Beloved, with God, the whole court and my own people that in all my trouble I have not given Monsieur an angry word, nor reproached him in the least, or talked behind his back. On the contrary, I have made it my special study to bear with him and not to say anything that would displease him, and when he has taunted me I have kept as still as a mouse while I might have thrown up his dead wife to him, although I, more than any one else, believe that happened without his knowledge. I said once, as he taunted me, that my chagrin would kill me, and I would die by my own violence. There would not be any greater trial in death, and I do not care enough for life to fear it; that is all I have said on this subject to Monsieur. I hope, my Ever Beloved, that you will not entertain so mean an opinion of me as to believe that I have been so unhappy through caprice and ill-humor alone. If I thought that you and uncle could believe such a thing of me, it would make me more melancholy than all my trouble hitherto."

## CHAPTER II.

### MATRIMONIAL PROJECTS.

IN the earlier part of the correspondence, the cares and anxieties of the young mother, also, form a part of the theme. Madame was very anxious for the safety of her babies, for, as she said, they had such a singular way of treating them in France, and, unfortunately, she herself had no experience. If she could but send the little Duc de Chartres to her dear Frau Von Harling in a letter, she could be assured that he would receive the care for which she herself was so grateful to her old governess. She had no confidence in the physicians, who, as she thought, understood nothing of the care of infants and would listen to nothing that was said to them. They had sent a lot of children into the other world, five of the Queen's and three of Monsieur's. She knew this because he had told her himself. Alas! her fears were only too well grounded, for she was soon called upon to mourn the loss of her first-born, the little Duc de Valois, then three years old. The distress of the mother was pitiful, but, supposing him to have resembled his brother, one can now hardly regret that another "Regent" was not left in the world.

Two children remained, the Duc de Chartres, afterward the infamous ruler of France during the minority of Louis XV., and a daughter. After this the mother was permitted to centre her devotion upon these two who lived and thrived. On the tenth of October, 1676, she had written: "The Duc de Chartres, thank God, is in perfect health, and his sister also is as fat as a stuffed goose and very large for her age. Last Monday they were baptized and given the names of Monsieur and myself, so the rogue is called Philippe and his sister, Elizabeth Charlotte. As there is now another 'Lieschen' in the world, God grant that she may not be more unhappy than I, and that she will not have as much cause to complain."

Matrimonial plans in behalf of her step-daughters soon engrossed Madame's attention. She seems to have been fond of them and very anxious to see them well married. She would have liked to marry one of them to the Dauphin, but received no encouragement in that quarter, and a marriage was shortly arranged for him with the Princess of Bavaria, whom Madame had heard was both ugly and delicate. The Princess of Orleans was married to the King of Spain very much against the wishes of her step-mother. Madame was not favorably impressed by the bridegroom, and did not want her step-daughter to go to what she considered a dreadful country. Unhappily her fears were justified, for history repeated itself, and the unfortunate princess perished under conditions very similar to those which had caused the tragic death of her own mother.

Monsieur's other daughter married Victor Amadeus, Duke of Savoy and first King of Sardinia.

The settlement of her own children soon proved a source of great anxiety to Madame. She became aware of a plan which she believed was instigated, or, at least, strongly favored by Madame de Maintenon, to marry her son to Mademoiselle de Blois, a natural daughter of the King by Madame de Montespan. Madame de Maintenon was now the power behind the throne, Queen of France, indeed, in all but in name. Her influence over the King was absolute, and it was more than suspected that she was his legal wife. Her present elevation was, indirectly, due to the children of Madame de Montespan, as it was her position as their governess which first brought her into the notice and favor of the King. She was, moreover, deeply attached to these children, and always sought, as did the King himself, to advance them in every possible way. Madame first mentioned her knowledge of this matrimonial project in a letter to her aunt the Electress, written April 11, 1688. The letter was sent by the hand of a trusted messenger, for Madame would not have dared to confide its contents to the post. As may be imagined, the scheme was contemplated by her with extreme displeasure. At this time the Duc de Chartres was but fourteen years of age, and as the marriage with Mademoiselle de Blois was not consummated until 1692, four years afterward, Madame had ample time to anticipate the dreaded *mésalliance* and to form plans to avert it.

Her position was rendered the more difficult in that she dared not speak to her husband of the matter, for fear, as she said, he would follow his usual custom and tell the King. Madame de Caylus said that Monsieur was really pleased with the idea. It was supposed that the Duc de Chartres was in love with Madame la Duchesse, and once Madame de Caylus referred to this when talking to Mademoiselle de Blois, who answered: "I do not care whether he loves me, only that he marries me." As Madame de Caylus grimly remarked, she had that satisfaction.

St. Simon, in his memoirs, gives a graphic account of the end of the affair. He relates that when the King was ready to broach the matter he sent for Monsieur and obtained his consent before the young Duc de Chartres was summoned to his presence. Madame had extracted from her son a promise that he would never consent to the match. When in the royal presence, however, the youth was overpowered by the manner of the King, as he told him his wishes, professing meanwhile to have no desire to constrain him. The young man replied that he had no will in the matter but would abide by the decision of his parents, thus throwing the responsibility upon them. The King then said that he had obtained Monsieur's consent, and, turning to his brother for confirmation, sent for Madame. When she appeared the King informed her that he had the consent of her husband and son to the marriage, and it only remained for her agreement to ratify the arrangement. Madame, seeing there was no help for it, cast one angry glance at her husband and son, and, bowing slightly, murmured that she would acquiesce in whatever they desired. Once out of the royal presence, however, she gave vent to her feelings and would listen to no explanation from Monsieur or her son.

That evening there was the usual assemblage of the court which occurred three times a week. The King sent for Monsieur, Madame, the Duc de Chartres, and Mademoiselle de Blois. Poor little Mademoiselle de Blois, who was not yet accustomed to attend these functions, feared that she had been sent for to be reprimanded, and trembled so that Madame de Maintenon took her on her knees to reassure her. Then the announcement was made and was received by the courtiers with surprise and consternation. It was just at this moment that St. Simon arrived upon the scene. The courtiers were standing about in groups discussing the affair, Monsieur looked very crestfallen, Madame visibly angry, and the Duc de Chartres very ill at ease and with eyes red with weeping. Madame soon retired to the gallery outside, where she strode along accompanied by one of her favorites, her handkerchief in her hand, weeping and talking loudly with wild gesticulations. At supper that night, the King offered her the different dishes, but she rudely repulsed his polite attempts to propitiate her. As they rose from the table he made her a low bow, but Madame, executing a pirouette, presented only her back when he raised his head. The next morning when the court was assembled to wait for the breaking up of the council and the King's mass, Madame was in the gallery, when her son approached to kiss her hand as was his custom, but, as he did so, she gave him a sounding box on the ear.

Long afterward, when time had not reconciled her either to the birth or the personality of her daughter-in-law, she wrote: "If I could have given my rank to have prevented the marriage, I would have done so." This was putting it as strongly as possible, for nothing was more characteristic of Madame than the high value she placed upon rank.

Aside from her birth, Mademoiselle de Blois does not seem to have been a desirable *parti*. St. Simon described her, in after life, as being majestic in appearance, but it is difficult to conceive it, for she had a deformity of figure which caused her to walk awry. Her complexion is said to have been good, but her cheeks were too full and overhanging, her nose long, and her teeth, also, too long. Her pride was so great that, preposterous as it was, she evidently considered that she, the daughter of a king, had conferred a favor on the Duc de Chartres by marrying him. She treated her husband coldly, and he frequently referred to her as "Madame Lucifer."

Madame never could see any good in her daughter-in-law, although, to do her justice, she seems to have determined to make the best of it. She adored her son, and his welfare was ever, with her, a matter of paramount importance. She had so strong a sense of what was due to the dignity of the family that she was always on the alert to avoid public scandal, but no family ever could have given greater cause for apprehension on that score. Madame was exasperated by seeing her husband openly pillaged by his favorites, her daughter-in-law was a constant annoyance, and her son had already begun to display the bad habits which afterward rendered him so notorious.

Her daughter gave her less uneasiness, but at twenty she was yet unmarried and her mother was looking about for a husband for her. Madame described her as not pretty, but nice-looking, with a good figure and half a head taller than herself. She would rather have had King William for a son-in-law, than the Emperor of Germany, who was then a widower. She feared, however, that Elizabeth would have to remain a spinster, as to all appearance the King was going to marry a Danish princess. She thought the Emperor would take the second Princess of Savoy and the Duke of Lorraine the daughter of the Emperor, so there would be nothing left. A marriage was afterward arranged with the Duke of Lorraine, and the mother was satisfied, although she dreaded the parting, and in the days preceding the wedding described herself as going about with a full heart and more ready to weep than to laugh. They had never been separated and now were to part for a long time.

It has been said that the daughter was not ill pleased to escape from the strict rule of her mother, but be that as it may, the mother always expressed the greatest tenderness, although, as she said, she was obliged to conceal her feelings lest people should laugh at her, for in France they could not comprehend how people could love their relations.

The following year, Madame referred to a proposed journey to Lorraine, which had to be given up because the etiquette of the reception of herself and Monsieur could not be arranged satisfactorily to the King. The Duke claimed the right of sitting in an armchair when in their presence, as he said the Emperor of Germany had allowed him this privilege. Louis's idea of etiquette was different, however, and Monsieur and Madame had to stay at home.

The Duke and Duchess of Lorraine seem to have lived peaceably together, at least the Duchess, who was of an amiable disposition, was so fond of her husband that she forgave his infidelities and he thus found it easy to make his peace with her. After his death, her high qualities having endeared her to the people, she was made Regent.

## CHAPTER III.

### MONSIEUR AND MADAME.

MONSIEUR, the husband of Madame, is described as a short, portly man, with dark hair and eyes, a long face and large nose, always dressed and be-ribboned in the most elaborate fashion. His hands were covered with rings, and he was even suspected of applying a little rouge to his face. St. Simon ungallantly said that his faults were those of women. One of them, his inability to keep a secret, has been mentioned, and once, the witty Duc, to indicate Monsieur's condition when very much out of sorts, said that he talked less than usual, indeed "Not more than three or four women." He had displayed an admirable courage in the battle-field, but in times of peace his tastes were essentially feminine. He was not fond of the chase, and as Madame said: "If it were not in time of war, he never in his life could bring himself to mount a horse. He wrote so badly that frequently be brought me letters that he had written and said, laughingly: 'Madame, you are accustomed to my writing, read me a little of that, I don't know what I have written.' We have often laughed heartily about it. In the army they said of him, that he feared the sun and the dust more than the guns of the enemy."

With all his shortcomings, however, Monsieur possessed considerable dignity and grace of manner, an inheritance from his mother, Anne of Austria, and like her he knew how to entertain and to hold a court.

St. Simon described his residence at St. Cloud as a veritable palace of delights, where everything possible was done for the pleasure of the guests. In their entertainment, Madame gave Monsieur no assistance as she was constantly shut up in her room, the walls of which she had hung with portraits of German princes, writing her interminable letters. From these letters, however, some light is thrown upon her apparently churlish behavior, for in one of them she said: "One soon regrets having said frankly what one thinks; see, why I live so much alone."

Indeed, this very outspoken princess could hardly have mingled much with the people about her without rendering herself more unpopular than she was already. The safest course was to take refuge in solitude. Her honest and upright soul was sickened by the deceit and treachery of the time-serving courtiers. She was shocked by the gossip and scandal so freely circulated, although she permitted herself to retail it to her correspondents, and we get from her letters but a sorry impression of the civilization and morality of the period.

But,—it was two hundred years ago, and these people were brought together under the influence of all the elements that tend to debase human nature. Enervated by luxury, tempted by idleness, and corrupted by the example of the King himself, were they so much worse than people living under like conditions now? When, to-day, the veil that propriety has drawn over the comedy of high life, is thrust aside, do we not sometimes have a revelation which strongly recalls the good old days of Louis Quatorze?

The two persons who have made us most intimately acquainted with the life of that period are the Duc de St. Simon and Madame. The former, the polished courtier and man of the world, who yet seems to have kept himself untainted by the vices of his associates, looked with amused interest upon the play going on around him, the players meanwhile having no suspicion that they were to be impaled upon the needle of his sarcastic wit and held up for the warning of future generations.

Madame, on the other hand, looked with ill-concealed disapprobation on the people she was compelled to live among, and although she cultivated a cheerful spirit, seems to have taken little pleasure in society and to have made her correspondence the chief business of her life. Any interruption of this favorite pursuit was regarded with the greatest impatience. The visits of the great ladies of the court she considered a tiresome waste of the precious time set apart for the answering of letters. These letters numbered, as she once stated, four every day and twelve on Sunday. It may easily be imagined that she was not a favorite, and it is probable that had the people of the court not been under the necessity of paying respect to a person of her rank, she would have been left severely alone.

Madame's personal appearance was far from prepossessing, if we are to judge from the description of contemporaries, and from her own, which she gave to her sister the Countess Amelie Elizabeth, as follows:

"I have to laugh heartily, dear Amelie, that you find in the portrait I sent to my aunt, that I look well and pretty. If a broad face, flat mouth, and little narrow eyes are pretty, then I am certainly, and grow every day prettier, because I grow broader every day.

"Dearest Amelie, every one must follow his destiny; mine has brought me to France; there I have lived, and there I must also die. Germany is to me always dear, and I am so little fitted for France that my whole life in the court is passed in the greatest solitude. Meanwhile, I see that it is God's will that I am here and that I should stay here; I have surrendered myself to that. I am very much obliged to you for longing for me: it must be your good heart as well as your race that causes that in you. There are many things in the world that one might long for but that through the understanding are impossible; so it is with me also."

That Madame's personal attractions were not augmented by art, we may gather from what she said of her wardrobe while yet a young woman: "I do not see why it is necessary to have so many costumes; mine consist of my court dress and a hunting costume when I ride; I have no others. I have never in my life had a *robe de chambre*."

St. Simon corroborated this singular statement, and said that during sixty years Madame had never worn the last-named garment, which, owing to her good health, she had little use for, but that she was always going about in a man's peruke and a riding-habit, except when in court dress. This lack of choice once led to Madame's appearance in an elaborate costume at an inopportune time, as St. Simon entertainingly relates. At the death of Monseignior, the first Dauphin, the court had been hastily summoned, upon the sudden alarm, and was gathered in the Salon at Versailles, its members in various stages of undress, when Madame appeared, late, but arrayed in full court dress, inundating everybody with her tears, and starting the lamentations afresh by her cries.

It was, perhaps, in keeping with Madame's custom, to think little of her dress, but much of what was due to her position. She said of herself: "All my life since my youth I have found myself so ugly that I have never been tempted to adorn myself much. Jewels and fine toilets only attract attention to the people who wear them. It is well that I was in that humor, because the late Monsieur, who loved adornment exceedingly, would have had a thousand quarrels with me to decide who should wear the finest diamonds. Never have I adorned myself but that he ordained my toilet entirely. He himself put the rouge upon my cheeks." This last device of vanity was not, however, approved by Madame, who commented severely upon the practice of many ladies of the court, who smeared their faces with a white preparation, which she had refused to allow Monsieur to apply to her face when he wished to do so. In general she seems to have declined to use any artifice to improve her looks.

One of the principal foes to beauty in that day was smallpox, and few of the royal family escaped its ravages. Madame's face was disfigured by the disease. Her complexion was, moreover, affected by the exposure to which her passion for outdoor exercise subjected her. But, as she said : " I have never desired to be handsome, and have never troubled myself about my skin, otherwise I would not, during thirty years, have followed the chase as I have done." And also, when writing to the Countess Louise :

" Is it possible, dear Louise, that you have never seen a race-hunt ? I have seen more than a thousand stags taken, and I have also had many good falls. In twenty-six times that I have fallen from my horse, I was only injured once, and that was not from racing ; I only found a stone under my elbow that dislocated my arm. From none of my other falls did I carry away the least hurt—that is why I dote on racing." And again : " I know well what it is to be exposed to a burning sun. It has happened to me many times to remain in the chase from morning until five o'clock—nine hours. I came in as red as a lobster, and with my face all burned. This is why I have such rough, brown skin. They do not pay any attention here to dust. I have known in our journeys such a dust that we could hardly see each other in the carriages, and meanwhile the King did not tell the cavaliers to keep a little farther away. The outdoor air never did me any harm. At Marly I often walked in the moonlight."

From the reference to the dust we get an idea of some of the minor discomforts of the court ladies during their frequent journeyings. As they were always going about from one place to another, often in full dress, the incidents by the way, when enveloped in dust or overturned in the mud, must have been, to say the least, somewhat annoying. Of one of these little occurrences, Madame wrote from Fontainebleau, as follows:

"I went out to drive in the forest as I do every day. Scarcely had we started when the coachman overturned us; one of my ladies was cut in the shoulder and side by broken glass. There were seven dogs in the carriage, but none of them suffered the least injury."

This *entourage* of pets was one of the fancies of these royal people. The King had sometimes as many as nine dogs in his cabinet and Madame was generally surrounded by seven or eight. This unhappy lady, however, needed all aids to diversion, for, as she wrote to the Countess Louise:

"If you knew everything that passes here you would certainly not be surprised that I am not gay. Another in my place would perhaps a long time ago have died of chagrin, but I only grow fat on it." At another time she said: "I have no need of consolation in regard to death, I do not desire, neither do I fear it. One can learn not to attach one's self too much to this world without the Catechism of Heidelberg, above all in a country where all is full of falseness, of envy and wickedness, and where the most unheard of vices spread without restraint, but to desire death is a thing totally opposed to nature; in the midst of this great court I retire as in a solitude. There are very few people that I have much to do with. For long days I am entirely alone in my cabinet, where I occupy myself in reading and writing. If any persons come to visit me, I see them for a moment, we talk of the rain or the fine weather or the news of the day, then I take refuge in my retreat. Four times a week I have my courier days, Monday to Savoy, Wednesday to Modena, Thursday and Sunday I write long letters to my aunt in Hanover. From six to eight I drive with Monsieur and our ladies. Three times a week I go to Paris, and every day I write to my friends who live there. I go to the hunt once or twice a week. It is thus that I pass my time."

## CHAPTER IV.

### THE DEATH OF MONSIEUR.

THE ill-assorted union of Monsieur and Madame was terminated by the death of Monsieur in June, 1701, but the unhappy Princess found herself in a position of no greater freedom than before. At first, she was in a state of great apprehension as to her future, because according to her marriage contract she was, upon the death of Monsieur, either to enter a convent or go to live at the Château de Montargis. St. Simon gave a graphic account of the scenes attending the death of Monsieur, and described Madame, in the midst of her grief, crying out:

"No convent; let no one speak of a convent!" Nothing would have been farther from her taste, and it was no wonder that her liveliest fears were aroused. She had the greater cause for anxiety as the King had recently shown a marked coolness toward Monsieur and herself. Madame had been ill for six weeks before the death of Monsieur and the King had not been near them. This was contrary to his usual custom, for, as St. Simon said, he was accustomed to go to them whenever either suffered from the most trifling indisposition.

On the day preceding Monsieur's death, the brothers had an interview which terminated in a furious quarrel, and it was thought that the anger of Monsieur might have brought on the fatal attack of apoplexy which seized him in the evening. Even then the King hesitated about going to him, and went only when told, in the middle of the night, that his brother was in imminent danger. All this was not reassuring to Madame, and, shortly after the death of Monsieur, she sent for Madame de Maintenon to come and see her, desiring to find out in what way she had offended the King, and also to assure herself as to her future fate. St. Simon wrote an account of the curious interview, as given him by an eye-witness, an occasion on which Madame de Maintenon in her cold-blooded way scored a little triumph over the proud Princess.

After Madame had desired to know why the King was displeased with her and had protested her innocence of having given him cause for the feeling, Madame de Maintenon drew from her pocket a letter which Madame had written to her aunt in Hanover. In this intercepted epistle Madame had commented very freely upon the relations between the King and Madame de Maintenon, and had also enlarged upon the unfortunate state of affairs throughout the kingdom.

Confounded by this evidence of her indiscretion, Madame could no longer deny having given cause of offence and was profuse in her apologies. She then essayed to make peace with Madame de Maintenon, whom she assured of her friendship, and, thinking she was on safe ground here, charged with having received her advances coldly. Madame de Maintenon permitted her to continue her protestations of friendship for a little, and then repeated some particularly offensive remarks which Madame had made to the late Dauphine concerning herself. Madame de Maintenon had never mentioned it before, but now ten years had elapsed and she thought that the death of the Dauphine absolved her from the promise of secrecy made at the time. Madame had trusted entirely in the fidelity of her late confidante, and, overwhelmed by this disclosure, sat like a statue, while Madame de Ventadour, who had remained with them during the interview, exerted herself to talk in order to give Madame time to recover herself. The interview finally terminated with the assurance from Madame de Maintenon that neither the King nor herself bore any malice on account of what had passed, and that they were willing to accept Madame's apologies. The ladies then parted with renewed promises of friendship.

Despite the protestations wrung from Madame during this embarrassing interview, however, we can hardly believe that her feelings toward Madame de Maintenon had undergone any change. The part the "Allmächtige Dame," as Madame called her, had played in arranging the marriage of the Duc de Chartres had never been forgiven by his mother, and this interview could only have intensified the hatred which she did not dare to show.

The all-powerful lady appears in Madame's letters under various epithets, perhaps most frequently under what might be translated "the old thing," and sometimes Madame's pen descends to a coarser word. In a letter written to the Countess Louise after the death of the King she gave her own version of the attempted reconciliation and also the reasons which seem amply to justify her dread of going to Montargis, as follows:

"After the death of Monsieur, the King caused me to be asked where I would go, into a convent or to Maubisson, or where. I replied that since I belonged to the royal family I could not live elsewhere than where the King was, and that I wished to go straight to Versailles. That pleased the King; he came to me; meanwhile it annoyed me a little because he had asked me where I wanted to go, because he had not thought that I wanted to remain where I was. I said that I did not know who had given His Majesty false reports concerning me, and that I had more respect and attachment for His Majesty than all those who had falsely accused me. Then the King made everybody go out, and we had a grand explanation, during which the King reproached me with hating Madame de Maintenon. I said it was true that I hated her, but it was only from my attachment to him, and because of the bad offices she performed for me with His Majesty. Meanwhile, I added, if it was agreeable to him, I was ready to be reconciled to her. The good lady did not foresee that, otherwise she would not have let him come near me. He was so sincere that he was favorable to me until his last moment. He had the old lady come to him and said to her: 'Madame wishes to be reconciled to you.' He made us embrace, and that ended the matter. He wished that afterward she should live peaceably with me; that was what she did outwardly, but she played me all sorts of underhand tricks.

"It would not have been disagreeable for me to go to Montargis, but I did not wish that it should have an air of disgrace as if I had committed some misdemeanor and had been sent away from court. It was to be feared also that two days from here they would let me die of hunger, and that did not suit me; I would rather be reconciled to the King. As to the retreat to a convent, that was not at all to my taste, but that was just what the old one would have desired. The Château de Montargis is my dower; at Orleans there is no house; St. Cloud is a piece of property that

Monsieur bought with his own money. Now my dowry is nothing. All that I have to live on comes from the King and my son; they left me without paying me anything at the beginning of my widowhood, at least they owed me three hundred thousand francs that they did not pay me until after the death of the King. Where would I have been if I had chosen my retreat at Montargis?"

St. Simon thought that Madame and her son were prodigiously well treated, Madame having a handsome allowance, with the Palais Royal, St. Cloud, and other residences, while the Duc de Chartres had his allowance augmented and was given the title of Duc d'Orleans, with all the perquisites of his father, and permitted to live in the same state. All this, as St. Simon said, was an unheard-of honor which had never been given to any other than a son of France before.

Although in the death of Monsieur, who had done so much for its entertainment, the court suffered a loss of gaiety and pomp which was felt for a long time, this event made scarcely a break in its ordinary amusements. The morning after his death, some one entering the apartments of Madame de Maintenon, where were the King and the Duchesse de Bourgogne, heard them singing together snatches of an operatic prologue, and after dinner, just twenty-six hours after Monsieur had ceased to breathe, play was resumed in the Salon by request of the King. The King was growing old, he was two years older than Monsieur, and those around him exerted themselves to keep him amused. Just at this time especially they wished to prevent him from feeling too deeply the reminder of his own mortality. Madame de Maintenon was always on the alert to provide him diversion and depended greatly upon the young Duchesse de Bourgogne[1] for aid in entertaining him. The young Du-

[1] Marie Adelaide, Princess of Savoy, who had been married to the Duc de Bourgogne, grandson of Louis XIV. The Duchesse de Bourgogne, grandniece of Monsieur by marriage, was also his granddaughter, as her mother was his daughter by his first marriage.

chesse really grieved for Monsieur, but she was not permitted to give way to the melancholy incited by his death.

Madame wrote afterward: "I had entirely won over my husband during the last years of his life. I brought him to laugh with me at his weaknesses, to take all pleasantly without being irritated. He would not suffer any one around him to calumniate or to attack me. He had in me a genuine confidence. He always took my part, but formerly I suffered horribly. I was just on the point of becoming happy when our Lord God took my poor husband away, and I saw disappear in one instant, the result of all the pains and care I had taken to become happy during thirty years."

We can scarcely believe, however, that the grief of Madame was very great. In forty days she was permitted to visit the King in full widow's costume, but she soon discarded the mantle and widow's cap, on the plea that the King did not like to see such sombre costumes about him and that the cap made her head ache. St. Simon seemed to be somewhat scandalized to see her appearing at certain public functions as soon as she did, and Madame herself naïvely regretted, to one of her correspondents, that she was not permitted to go to the play. The following winter, however, she was allowed to go to the apartments of Madame de Maintenon where comedies were played before the King. Madame expressed her feeling about the wearing of mourning once, as follows:

"When one comes into mourning, one can not get out of it again. I have, unfortunately, only too well experienced this. Nothing in the world changes the disposition more or makes one so melancholy. One becomes only the more sorrowful from something which calls attention to it; meanwhile, one cannot change it. That one is mortal one's self also, is not at all comforting. I have known for some years an old lady here, called Madame de Fiennes, who is very natural. Once, somebody of her acquaintance died, Madame de Fiennes wept bitterly.

Some one said to her: 'It did not appear that you loved the person who has just died, so much, during her life. Why do you weep now that she is dead?' Madame de Fiennes answered: '*Mon Dieu!* but you are foolish to think that I am weeping for that person. It is not for her that I weep, but for myself, since I must die as well as she, and her death has made me think of it.' By this you see, dear Louise, that few people can take death for a consolation."

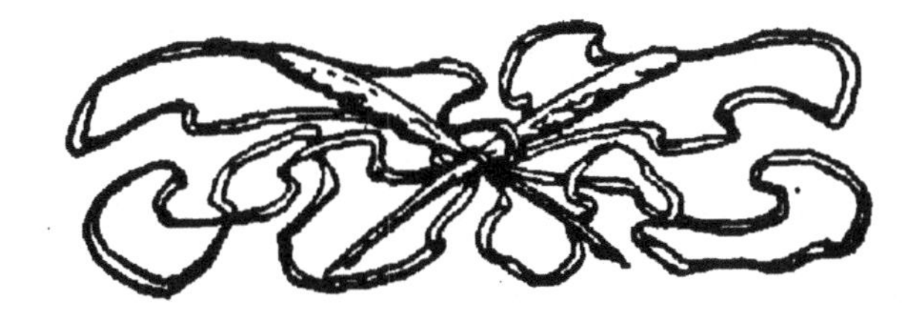

# CHAPTER V.

## THE RELIGION OF MADAME.

MADAME dearly loved "The Comedy," and as a means of grace placed her favorite recreation far above listening to a poor sermon. In a letter to the Countess Amelie Elizabeth, written from Versailles December 9, 1705, she expressed her opinion on the subject as follows:

"*La Mort de Pompée* is a beautiful piece, *Le Baron de la Crasse* right clever. *Le Lever du Roi*, as they call it here, is very naturally written as things go with us. I can not agree with you about the serious plays. The play is very badly recited when they speak as if they were reading; they should go through the movements as one would feel the passion. When they were moved by passion, as they all were in the serious comedies of Corneille, it was more to be praised. In the church one learns, but unpleasantly; in the play, however, instruction is given agreeably, as virtue is rewarded and vice punished. To listen a whole hour to a fellow shouting by himself, whom one may not contradict, may be very good, but it is not pleasant."

Madame's religious ideas were extremely simple and practical. She had entered the Roman Church upon her marriage with Monsieur, but her conversion had been too precipitate to be genuine, and she always remained at heart a Protestant, although sometimes she undertook to defend her adopted faith, as once when writing to the Countess Amelie Elizabeth:

"I have had so much to do every day with church going and often much to write that it was impossible to answer your letter.

"Are you so simple as to believe that the Catholics have no true ground of the Christian faith? Believe me, the ground of Christianity is with all the Christian religions the same. As to the difference, it is only the wrangling of the priests, that honest people don't concern themselves with; but what does concern us is to live well and in a Christ-like manner, to be merciful, and to be diligent in virtue. The priests should try to impress that upon Christians and not trouble themselves about their understanding every little point of doctrine, but that would lessen the authority of these gentlemen. For that reason they concern themselves about them and not what is most important and noteworthy." For herself, Madame said, that when she came to France, they made her hold conferences with three bishops who, as she found, had three different opinions, and that from these three opinions and from the Bible she had formed her religion. She best illustrated her position, however, by a little story which she related to her Aunt Sophia:

"It is certain that people lose religion and the fear of God in a wonderful manner. I have no faith in it all, and it will soon be with me as with an Englishman called Fielden. At Fontainebleau some years ago, Wendt said to him, 'Are you a Huguenot, sir?' 'No,' said he. 'Are you a Catholic?' said Wendt. Again the Englishman answered, 'Far from it.' 'You are a Lutheran.' 'Not at all,' said Fielden. 'What are you, then?' said Wendt. 'I will tell you,' said the Englishman. 'I have a little religion of my own.' So I believe I also have a little religion of my own. The good King James would have been better off if he had had the same rather than to lose three kingdoms through bigotry."

Madame liked Lutheran hymns, and used sometimes to sing them in her own room. As she said: "I believe the Reformers are sincere not to let themselves be carried away to believe what they cannot believe and that were it not for the sermon and psalms they might be drawn away; the psalms are not so unpleasant to hear as the vowels. In a high mass to hear nothing but a bawling of *a, a, a, a; e, e, e, e; i, i, i, i; o, o, o, o,* makes me so impatient that I would willingly run out of church on account of it, and while I stay, do it with a very bad grace. I do not believe that our dear, blessed Prince Karl would have found them more agreeable than the psalms, because they have a pretty melody. I thank Dr. Luther right heartily to have made pretty songs. I believe there is something pleasant in being Lutheran because it is something cheerful, but the mystics with their contemplation are not at all to my taste."

Madame also read every day in the German Bible. Going to church was, however, a great trial to her and almost invariably the sermon put her to sleep, but, as she said, "They have not reprimanded me for sleeping in church. I have grown so accustomed to it that I cannot break myself of it.

When they preach in the morning I do not sleep, but in the afternoon, it is impossible to keep from it. At the play I do not sleep, but often at the opera. I believe that the Devil troubles himself very little whether I sleep in church or not, because sleeping is a matter of indifference; it is no sin, but only a human weakness. We see few preachers who have the art of extinguishing our passions. If they are strong, they are our masters; if weak, we master them. But *messieurs* the preachers take nothing therefrom and add nothing thereto. They are human like ourselves, and have enough to do to look after themselves. When you preach, dearest Amelie, I promise not to sleep under your sermon, and as you are a cheerful Christian I hope you will beguile the way with music. This is not a bad prayer, to have a cheerful spirit. One sees in this country as much wickedness that is happy as sad; one cannot judge from that. Our God gives the temperament; time and age do much thereafter. I was more cheerful when I was young. Now

I am rather always weary." And again, in writing to the Electress Sophia: "For the rest, I could wish from the bottom of my soul, that all the devotees (I should rather have said bigots) here might follow your preaching, so that union and peace might be brought about. But no one here follows your maxims at all, for each is set against the other, husband against wife, father against son, servants against their masters, and what more may be to place them in an unhappy and unfortunate state, one might well say as in that piece with the old Rabenhaupt, '*Bon jour, Monsieur,* you are living with the Devil.' There is another old German proverb, which I can very well understand, which says that when the Devil cannot enter in, he sends an old woman, which we all in the royal family very well know. But enough of this; more would not be advisable."

Writing to the Countess Amelie Elizabeth from Versailles, February 17, 1704, Madame said: "What nonsense is this, that they suspect about what you write to me from Frankfurt? Do you mean that they confide to you all the town affairs, that they fear you will reveal them to me? They might see your letters, then they would find that we don't speak of any town secrets, so they might as well allow our letters to go. I confess I am often surprised to hear how things go on in Germany. All must have changed frightfully in the thirty-two years that I have been here. When there are so many people in Frankfurt I wonder that they did not divert themselves better at the late Carnival. In Hanover, they make themselves very gay. God grant that it may last long and that they may keep in good health. I agree with you, dear Amelie, that one can do without amusement if one's time is only passed in peace and without annoyance; everything in this world does not go smoothly, vexation comes more often than joy. You would be a good preacher, dear Amelie. All that you have said was as good as a Lenten sermon, and I did not go to sleep over it, as I do over all other preaching here; for they go to the sermon half an hour after dinner, and it is impossible to keep myself from going to sleep, and there is not a sermon that I do not fall asleep over; to-day I slept so that my head nodded." And on February 25, 1705:

"I am very much indebted to you for praising me, although I know myself too well to think there is much in me that is praiseworthy; rather let me speak of something else than what I should be but am not. Your dear letter is too eloquent for me. Our Carnival is now past; I had to mask myself the last day, in my old days. My masquerade was merely a green taffeta, then I had upon a forked stick a great rosette of rose-colored ribbon. The taffeta was open from the head to the stomach. I had slipped into this with my clothes on. I fastened it at the neck and took the stick in my hand. They did not see my figure, and from my height I appeared small, and nobody knew me. I made the King very impatient because, as soon as he saw me, I bent the stick as if one made a courtesy to him. At last he became wholly out of patience, and said to the Duchesse de Bourgogne, 'Who is this great masque who salutes me every moment?' She laughed, and said to him at last, 'It is Madame.' I thought he would make himself ill laughing at my masquerade. I played him a trick also. They carried me away to dance, and I took the King. . . . It is a very annoying thing to sleep where there is a ball. I know what that is. I withdrew at twelve as usual to go to bed, although from four, when the ball was over, until all had left, which was two good hours, I found it impossible to sleep."

In her old age, when she lived in Paris, Madame gave up going to church after dinner, as she could not help going to sleep, and snored so loudly that she feared it might disconcert the preacher, especially as she sat in an arm-chair in front of the pulpit. From Marly, in 1705, she wrote: " . . . Also, I never pray from a book, in the church, I make all my prayers myself. . . . There is no Carthusian monk who lives a more lonely and quiet life than I. I believe I will end by forgetting how to talk if I do not talk more than I have done. The Frau von Rathsamhausen comes this evening or to-morrow morning; with her I go over the old histories of our youth. I will tell you here about my life. Every day, except Sunday and Thursday, I get up at nine, then I kneel and say my prayers and read my psalm and chapter in the Bible, then I wash myself as clean as I can, then I ring and my women come and dress me; by a quarter of eleven I am through, then I read or write. At twelve I go to mass, which lasts half an hour; after the mass, I talk with my own or with other ladies. At one precisely we go to the table. As soon as I come from dinner I walk up and down in my room for a quarter of an hour. Then I sit down at my table and write. At half-past six I call my ladies and go for an hour, or an hour and a half, for a walk, then back to my room until supper. Is not that a hermitage? Sometimes I go to the hunt, that lasts an hour, two at the most; and then again to my room. After the hunt I am all alone in my carriage, and I often sleep when the hunt does not go well. They sup at eleven; at a quarter to twelve they leave the table; then I wind my clocks, put my things from my pocket into a basket, and undress myself."

From Versailles, February 3, 1705, Madame wrote to the Countess Amelie Elizabeth: "My dearest Amelie, I am right glad you liked the little silver box, but it did not merit being prized as a rarity, for it is not that at all. Louise and you have not given each other anything at New Year, I see, so this is the first present you have had this year. Do you carry tobacco in a bag? That was not what I meant. It is a hateful fashion. I did not think you so much in the mode. From my heart I do not grudge your having been so very gay. I cannot say so much for myself. I eat the whole year through, all alone at midday. I hurry as much as possible, it is so annoying to eat alone with twenty fellows around one, seeing everything one puts in one's mouth, and counting every bite. I eat, therefore, in less time than half an hour. At night I eat with the King; there are five or six at table; each eats his own way as in a cloister, without any thing to say, unless a couple of words whispered to his neighbor."

As Madame remained thoroughly German in all things, she, naturally, detested French cookery. Of this she wrote: "I am all German as regards eating and drinking, and have been all my life. They cannot fry things well here, the milk and the butter are not as good as they are with us; they have no taste and are like water. The cabbages are not good, either, because the land is not rich, but light and sandy, so the vegetables have no strength and the cattle do not give good milk. *Mein Gott!* but I wish I could eat some of the dishes your cook makes for you, they would be more to my taste than all my *maître d'hôtel* prepares." Madame disliked soups, except beer soup and ragouts, and to the latter, which she said were nothing but bad messes made of broth and pepper and salt, garlic and onion mixed up, she preferred a good leg of mutton or a ham. A good dish of sauer-kraut and smoked sausages was, to her taste, better than all—a dish fit for a king. Upon one occasion she thanked her sister for a recipe of a dish concocted of sauer-kraut and fish, which, as she was not fond of fish, she did not care to try. She could endure neither tea, coffee, nor chocolate, and could not understand how people could bring themselves to the point of indulging in these foreign drinks. Coffee, in her opinion, was very injurious in its effects, and she had known of several instances in which it had caused death after horrible sufferings.

For doctors, Madame had little use. In a letter to the Countess Louise, she once expressed her attitude with regard to their services, as follows: "My cough is gone as I had thought; I trouble myself very little about the impatience of the doctors. As I have positively said to them before, they need not demand any blind obedience from me; they may speak their minds, but need not be vexed if I do not always follow their advice. My health, my life, is my own, and I will govern it as I see fit. The doctors must talk about their art to make themselves appear necessary, but I do not find them more learned than nature left to itself when it has help in need and time enough, and is not hindered by irresolution. The doctors can hardly cure sickness, how can they then prevent it. I admit that one needs them when one is ill, but I must really be ill before they can bring me to it. Bleeding I cannot stand, it takes away all my strength. I must be very ill before I will be bled."

Whatever the disease, bleeding was the first resort. As the Bourbons ate and drank enormously, this treatment of depletion may sometimes have proved beneficial in the royal family, but, considering the usual results of medical practice in those days, Madame's dread of physicians was well founded. Lives upon which the fate of empires hung were recklessly sacrificed, and the hygienic conditions which surrounded these people were probably little better than those from which the poorest suffer in our day. Contagious diseases in their worst forms raged unchecked, carrying off their victims from among the highest in station, and almost exterminating the royal family itself. It is no wonder that malaria, from which even Madame with her rugged constitution did not escape, was a frequent ailment. Her thoughts went back to the beloved Palatinate, which she described as a land blessed above all others, where food, water, and air were all of the best. And once in writing of Heidelberg, she recalled one of the pleasures of her vanished youth in these words: "*Mein Gott*, how many times have I eaten cherries with a morsel of bread, on the mountain at five o'clock in the morning. I was more gay then than to-day."

## CHAPTER VI.

### THE DEATH OF THE ELECTRESS.

ABOUT this time Madame experienced one of the greatest sorrows of her life in the death of her aunt, the Electress Sophia, June 18, 1714. Madame had lived with her aunt nearly all her life, before her marriage, and was deeply attached to her.

The Electress had attained a good old age, greatly esteemed for her wit and judgment. She had lived to inherit the throne of England and had seen her son become ruler of that country in her place, under the title of George the First. Madame was the daughter of the eldest brother of the Electress, but was one of those excluded by the Act of Settlement, which gave the English crown to the Protestant descendants of Sophia, who was the granddaughter of James I. Madame, who otherwise would have been nearer the succession than her cousin George, did not regret that her change of religion had cut her off from this dignity. She averred that she would not trust a hair of her head to the English, whom she considered the most uncertain of people. She feared her cousin would regret his temerity in undertaking to reign over them instead of ruling in Hanover, where his power was absolute. She evidently thought he had taken his life in his hands, because there was no telling what to expect from a people who had the habit of treating their kings badly. If the King of England reigned as absolutely as his Majesty of France, she would have had no doubt that all would go well, but as it was, she was greatly troubled for the safety of her relative.

As to the stability of the throne of France,

no glimmering of events which were even then casting their shadows before, was perceived by Madame, so filled was her mind with a belief in the divine right of kings.

Her first letter after the receipt of the news of the Electress's death was from Marly, June 24, 1714.

"Dearest Louise, I await a letter from Hanover, in which to see that they have called you back on account of our, alas! great misfortune, and I can not doubt you are again in Hanover, therefore I write, not that I may console you, but that my tears which flow continually may mingle with yours. Our loss is unending, my weeping may cease, but my sorrow never. This dear Electress was my sole consolation in all the trials that have been put upon me here. When I complained to her late Highness and received an answer I was again consoled. Now I am as if all alone in the world. I believe our God sends this unhappiness in order to take away from me the sting of death, as it is now certain that I can end my life without sorrow and with nothing in this world to regret. My children are provided for, they have such consolation in this world that they can soon forget me, therefore I will not hold back when it is God's will to take me hence. If it would come to pass soon it would be a great boon, as it would end my pain. I would like, to-day, to answer your dear letter of the fourth of this month,that I received at Rambouillet, and which I have not answered before because I feared my letter would be lost while you were on a journey.

"I pray you, dear Louise, get all my packets, take out what is for you, read what I have written or not, keep and burn it afterward. And should Monsieur de Wersebé come with my packet, I pray you to read it and burn it, while you will see therefrom many things that perhaps you did not know. I believe our God caused you to go away in order to spare you this frightful shock, because what one hears is not so terrible as what one sees, while the trouble is all the same. I would wish to talk longer because it relieves the heart to speak with those who are in the same position as ourselves, but my head and eyes give me such frightful pain from much weeping that I hardly know what I say, so, much against my will, now close and say no more except that I will love you from my heart as long as my wretched life endures."

The packet referred to contained a letter from Madame to her aunt which had reached its destination after the latter's death. It had not been entrusted to the post, but had been sent by the hand of a messenger, and the writer was greatly disturbed for fear it might fall into the hands of the ministers, but to her intense relief it was afterward secured by the Countess Louise.

The Court was to go back to Versailles, and on October 20th, Madame wrote: "Dearest Louise, this is the last letter I shall write from dear Fontainebleau, because we go on Wednesday, and on Monday will be the last hunt in this beautiful forest. There is nothing to compare with it at Marly or

Versailles. What pleases me in this place is, that all the salons and galleries seem wholly German. When one goes into the Swiss salon, it seems exactly like an old German room with balconies and wainscoting and benches. I feel at once that the air here, as also the hunting, agree with me and give me good health; they drive away sad thoughts, and nothing is more injurious to my health than to be sad. Until now our hunts have passed off very well. Last Thursday, they caught a stag which was a little bad. A nobleman mounted a rock behind the stag and gave him a blow in the thigh; he could not buck his head, there was no danger. Behind my calêche was another containing three reverend gentlemen, the Archbishop of Lyons and two abbés, who were not used to the chase, and when the stag sprang towards them two of them sprang out of the calêche and got behind it and flattened themselves on the ground. I was very sorry not to have witnessed this scene, for I would have laughed heartily for we old hunters were not afraid of the stag. I made your compliment to the Electoral Prince at the hunt, and said to His Highness that you wished to assure him of your respect. He made me a deep reverence but answered nothing. I am not in his good graces. I believe he thought that I would speak to him upon religion and persuade him to change, while that did not happen at all. But the good gentleman deceived himself greatly, for I am no apostle, and find it good that every one should believe according to his understanding, and should people follow my advice there would be no quarrelling over religion, and they would persecute the crime and not the belief, and seek to improve it with correction. But the good Prince is so frightened that, without considering, all worries him. Hagen has encouraged me little to speak to his Prince. I have answered merely that I understood nothing of controversy and could only trouble myself about my own belief. Also the Prince did me an injustice to shun me so. I might, very probably, please him little because I am an old woman, but that is not likely to alter and every day grows worse. While this gentleman has not hitherto held fast to his religion, I cannot believe that he will ever change. No Bible has the Prince nor hymn book, he has only a book written in his own hand wherein he prays, so his people say. I do not believe that anything pleases him here except the hunting. He is shocked that the women here paint themselves so much. I know well how my aunt used to permit herself to say, through you, amusing things about the Electoral Prince. It is very droll when a Turk happens to adopt the Christian faith while he remains at heart a pagan still. That is hypocrisy, dear Louise. But in the Christian religion just to hold forth the Bible and to believe in one's heart what one can understand, that cannot be called hypocrisy. All Christians should be brothers, and it is the fault of the priests and through their ambition that in the Christian religion people are set one against another and discord made, and thus each one wants to rule in his religion and play the master.

"I seldom see the Electoral Prince because I have neither music, nor play, nor company of an afternoon. I live for myself and do not have many people about. Those I see, I treat as politely as ever I can, but great intimacy or familiarity have I with no one. I do not believe that the Prince will become acquainted with me. I see well that he shuns me. He speaks very little here, one must draw the words from him. He is handsome in appearance, has good manners and mien; the little that he says is well said and one sees that he has understanding and is agreeable when it pleases him. He pleases everybody here. That is what I have to say of the Electoral Prince of Saxony."

On November 3, 1714, Madame wrote from Versailles:

". . . I have read four pages and have not found the place, will look again directly, there . . . I have found it, dear Louise. They have reported my harangue in presenting the Electoral Prince very badly, for, firstly, I never in my life call the King, Sire, only Monsieur. What they call *enfants de France* do not call the King, Sire, that is for the *petits enfants de France*, as for example, my son, my daughter, etc. What I said to the King was only: '*Monsieur, voici le Prince Electoral de Saxe qui souhaite que je le présente à votre Majesté.*' The Prince stepped up with right high and good mien and made his compliment to the King without the least embarrassment and thereby won at once the approbation of the King and the whole court. The King answered him very politely. All went well. The Prince then presented his two governors, Count Cos and Baron Hagen, who also as well as their master gained the esteem of every one. If all the correspondence from France to Germany is no better than this about my presentation of the Electoral Prince, the correspondents do not earn their money. I have asked His

Highness, the Electoral Prince, if he awaited another governor, but he said he did not know a word about it.

"General Lutzenberg has a sister here, Madame des Alleurs. You know her perhaps, because her husband, who has just come from Turkey where he has been Ambassador, was awhile ago Ambassador at Berlin where you must have seen him in the late Queen's time. They have said that he was a little beloved by the beautiful Queen. Whenever I come across his wife, I will say that the General should take counsel of his sister because she has the understanding of the Devil. But I believe he would not remain so innocent of the propriety of this as he now is, were he not so guarded that neither man nor woman can speak to him. One cannot have more politeness than the Palatin from Lithuania. Monsieur Hagen, also, knows very well how to live and seems to be a fine man. I find him intelligent in all things except religion, there he is perfectly foolish. He was willing that

I should have spoken to his Prince, but I said to him that preaching did not come from women and that our God had not sent me as an apostle, therefore I would not speak to the Prince on religion. He holds himself as fast as a wall and will not be persuaded. They brought him to vespers day before yesterday, where he came as they were singing a psalm to music; he heard it through and when the music was done he ran out. When I see Monsieur Hagen, I will say to him how much of good you have written to me about his wife; that will please him because he loves her dearly.

"I thank you very much for the picture of the King of England. If this resembles him, he must have altered frightfully. I do not find a single feature of him, and the picture resembles the late good Monsieur Polier in his youth. And when this King was here he had a handsome face and not at all a large mouth; smallpox and time must have changed him very much. He had said to me through Monsieur Martine that so soon as he was in England he would write to me and have communication with me by letters. Yesterday, only, Monsieur Prior brought me a letter from his King but not in his own hand, merely through his secretary. That I had not expected after Monsieur Martine's compliment. When I think, however, how this King was always to me, I need not wonder much. He is the opposite of his mother. It may go as it will, I shall always remember that he is my aunt's son and for that reason wish him all luck and prosperity as I have also to-day written to him. I feel very sorry for the Princess of Wales, for my aunt was her consolation. I will not say more, but I esteem her much, for she has a good heart which is rare in these times. The tears came to my eyes when I read in your letter how movingly this Princess bade adieu to her children."

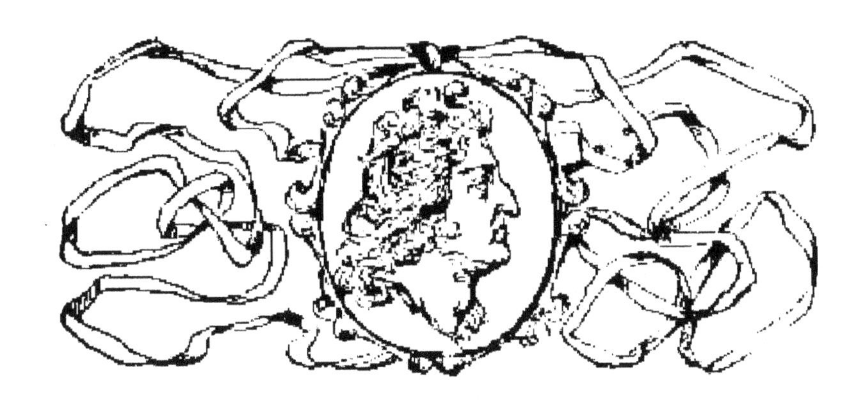

## CHAPTER VII.

### THE CLOSE OF THE REIGN OF LOUIS XIV.

IN the following year, August, 1715, Madame wrote from Versailles: "Dearest Louise, I have now a half hour to be in my room. That will I employ in entertaining you, although I am not at all more cheerful than I was last Tuesday, because our King is not well, alas! and it worries me so that I am half ill. I cannot eat or sleep well on account of it. God grant that I am wrong, but should the misfortune I fear come to pass, it will be the greatest I have experienced, and if I should speak of the matter it is something so frightful I cannot think of it without having my flesh creep. Say nothing to any one in England of what I say to you here. I am troubled to the depths of my soul." On the next day she wrote again:

"If you knew, dear Louise, how all is here, you would not wonder that I live so much alone. I cannot, neither do I wish to play, and people do not come willingly to those who do not play. Conversation is not in fashion any more, everybody is so timid and fears so much to talk that each shuns the other.

"I am a little old to run about with young people and those who are near my own age are with the all-powerful lady, whose favorite I am not at all, so I must stay alone, dear Louise. It does not trouble me much, because the company is rather distasteful to me than otherwise, when one cannot talk with open heart, but only about the weather or dress; that soon tires me and I would much rather be alone. There you see the reason of my solitude, and you will find, I think, that I am not wrong; with intrigues I can and will have nothing to do."

Madame never had taken much interest in gaming, the favorite pursuit of the court. She had never had the money to risk, nor the desire to enter into the amusement, in which, as she said, they played for frightful sums and became so excited that they acted as if demented. Monsieur, who was very fond of play, had not even wished that Madame should look on while he enjoyed himself in this way, as he thought it brought him ill luck. It was no wonder he felt so, for it was her money which gave him the opportunity, and, as she once said, it would not have made any difference had her people given her a larger portion, for Monsieur would only have had the more with which to gamble.

These were times of great uneasiness; the reign of Louis XIV., which had begun so auspiciously, was drawing to a disastrous close. Victory no longer perched upon the banners of France. There were unsuccessful foreign wars which drew away money greatly needed at home. Want and dissatisfaction prevailed among the people. There were winters so cold that the Seine was frozen over, and wood became so scarce that it was given in little bundles for New Year's gifts. The people, as Madame said, were dying like flies, and many hungry ones went about the streets crying for bread. They sometimes pursued the royal people with cries for food.

But there were other more threatening demonstrations against the Orleans family. Three heirs in the direct line of the royal succession had died: Monseigneur, the Dauphin; and recently his son, the second Dauphin, who bore the title of Duc de Bourgogne; and the eldest son of the latter, leaving only the second son, the little Duc d'Anjou, who was only five years old, as the successor of his great-grandfather Louis. The two last deaths, together with that of the Duchesse de Bourgogne, had occurred in quick succession and were, without doubt, caused by contagion aided by bad medical treatment. But the cry of poison was raised and popular suspicion fixed itself upon the Duc d'Orleans. There had been much talk and several very disagreeable public demonstrations.

The old King had been failing for some weeks and at last became worse. The last sacraments were administered and he took leave of the royal family. The dignity and self-control which had always distinguished him did not fail him, and he was able to pass through the last, long ordeal in an edifying manner. He gave the remaining members of his family his blessing and exhorted them to live in unity. Madame thought this advice was especially meant for her in her relations with her daughter-in-law, and hastened to assure him that as long as she lived she would endeavor to carry out his wishes. He laughed and said he had not intended his exhortation for her, but for the other Princesses. For her he expressed the tenderest affection, more than she had thought he felt for her, and said that he was sorry he had ever given her any trouble. She was touched to the last degree and, falling on her knees beside the bed, kissed his hands and wondered afterward how she had been able to pass through the trying scene without falling insensible. Madame said that the firmness of the King was wonderful, and that he had given orders and had arranged everything as if he had merely been going upon a journey.

Besides the loss of the King, however, Madame had a private cause of distress. Her son would become Regent and would go to Paris to live, and she must accompany him. This was not an agreeable prospect, for she disliked Paris exceedingly and was sure that to be shut up there where the air was bad would make her ill. In a letter written on the 27th of August, she informed the Countess Louise of the serious illness of the King, who had received the last sacrament the evening before, and said: "If the Master dies, as cannot be doubted, it is a greater misfortune for me than you could ever imagine, from many causes of which I cannot write. I cannot see what is before me but misery and misfortune; without vexation, discomfort, and weariness, I cannot live in Paris." On the 6th of September, she wrote to the Countess Louise from Versailles:

"Dearest Louise, it is a long time since I have written to you, but it has been impossible. I have been so overwhelmed and so deeply troubled that I could not write. I have spared my poor wet eyes to write to my daughter Friday and Tuesday. Our blessed King died last Sunday at half-past eight in the morning. You can well believe that I have had many visits to receive and pay, and many letters to receive and to write. I have to-day received your two dear letters of the 2d of September and the 22d of August; day before yesterday, also those of the 18th and 29th of August came, but I cannot to-day answer all, only the last. Really, I am now full of trouble, not only on account of the loss of the King but also because I must go to that cursed Paris for a whole year. Were I but ill I would go through and go to St. Cloud. *Mein Gott!* what would I endure for a pain! But complaining will not help the matter. It is better that I answer your dear letter. I am very frank; when anything goes to my heart, I must show it; until now it has not hurt me. It is true that it was a great consolation that the whole people, the troops, and the whole Parliament are for my son. His enemies, who deceived the King on his death-bed and caused him to make a will against my son, have been affronted; that my dear son had been openly declared Regent and that they with their cabal must give way. My son takes these things so frightfully hard that he has no rest night or day. I fear now that he will make himself ill over it, and many sad thoughts pass through my head of which I cannot speak. Also, sorrow is not now welcome. My son has himself openly spoken in Parliament and they have said it was not ill done. Thank Baron Goetz very much for his compliment. It pleases me that he is interested for me and mine. What you wish could happen without a miracle; the young King is very delicate. The ministers who were under the late King keep their places. Also it is not to be believed that they are less curious than they have been and so one may assure one's self that the letters will be opened. In Paris it is hardly possible that I can preserve my health without the air, exercise, hunting, and walking. In Paris I will have neither air nor exercise. What will come of it only time can show. What God wills, to that will I surrender myself, but the frightful wickedness and falseness of the world disgusts me with life. I cannot flatter myself that I am beloved of all the world."

A few days afterward she wrote from Paris:

"Ah, dear Louise, I do not wonder that our King's death went to your heart; what I wrote to you is not to be compared to what, unhappily, I heard and saw. The King himself was good and just, but the old woman had him so under her control that no one benefited by it, except her and his ministers, for he trusted nobody but her and his confessors and his ministers; and as the good man was not learned, so the Jesuit and the old woman instructed him in spiritual things, and the ministers, who were mostly bad enough, in worldly things. So I can truly say that what bad things happened did not come from the King. They instructed him to save his soul thereby, and you know, dear Louise, where one is persuaded of that, he can be very easily led. My eyes hurt me so from incessant weeping because I came away from Versailles. I have not wept without cause, for here I have truly an unquiet mind, I have not a moment's peace, as I am constantly interrupted. This morning I began to write at half-past nine when the interruptions commenced, and have continued until now, when it is half-past three. I cannot eat comfortably because I cannot take a bite in my mouth but must entertain all these people, and to eat alone is worse.

"It is true, dear Louise, that our King died on Sunday, the first of September at half-past eight. I have told you about it already, and how it went at the Parliament.

Yesterday they took the young King to the Parliament to have a Bed of Justice and my son's Regency became registered, secure and known. I can take my part and give myself up to God's will, but, dear Louise, how can one be cheerful or contented in constraint and discomfort. If it is God's will that I shall be unhappy until my end, so also must I submit. It cannot vex me that you should wish that I would not be sad, because I see well that it is only out of pure friendship, and that you fear that this trouble will make me ill.

"But should I become ill, it will be on account of the air of this place, because since last Monday when I came here, I have not been an hour free from headache.

"My son, I am sure, wishes that I might be happy here, but that is not in his power. It is only to be hoped that I will soon have a fever, because I have promised not to go away from here unless I am ill. Headache does not count, but I cannot be without that in Paris; if I have a fever, though, I will go to our dear St. Cloud. My son has many other things to think of beside my peace and pleasure.

"It seems to me he is resolved to live at peace with his neighbors. I believe, if it rested with my son, all evils would be relieved, but it is not possible to stop many things. To show that he does not rule through his own caprice alone, he has established several councils, one for the affairs of state, one for ecclesiastical matters, and one for foreign affairs, and another for war. Thus he can do nothing but what is herein decreed, and it is difficult to believe that the ecclesiastical council which is composed of priests will be very favorable to the Reformers. I have determined not to meddle with anything in the world. France has, unfortunately, as we know, been ruled by women much too long. As far as I am concerned I will not be the cause of the same being said of my son. I will give a good example that my son's eyes may be opened not to let himself be ruled by any woman whoever she may be.

"St. Cloud is to me a dear and lovely place because it is the most beautiful place in the world, but were I to go there now, all Paris would hate me, and as they have all shown so great an affection for my son and for me it is but right that I should deny myself for him. No, dear Louise, do not think that the death of the King has given me freedom as I would have liked. One must live according to the custom of the country, and has no choice; one must be in one's position a real victim of grandeur, and must do all the time what one does not like and but little as one wishes. You need not be much obliged to me for writing to you in my trouble, as nothing lightens the heart more than to complain of one's grief to those one loves and who take part in one's misfortune.

"It is true that every one thought the King dead when Madame de Maintenon went away; she thought so herself, but he had only a long fainting fit, and came to himself again and lived as I have said.

I will not talk more of these things, it pains me too much. The King was very firm in his last moments. He said, laughingly, to Madame de Maintenon: 'I thought death was harder than it is. I assure you it is not a great matter and does not seem hard to me.' Twice he remained twenty-four hours without speaking to any one. In that time he did nothing but pray, saying: 'My God, have pity on me. Lord, I am ready to appear before thee. Why, my God, dost Thou not take me?' Afterward, he repeated the Lord's Prayer devoutly and the creed and all prayers for the commending of the soul and giving his soul into God's hands."

# CHAPTER VIII.

## THE REGENT.

LOUIS XIV. was buried with scant ceremony. Verses upon the occurrence, of the most indecent and disrespectful character, were circulated, and little sorrow was shown by the people. They had suffered so much during the last years of his reign that any change was hailed as a deliverance. The Duc d'Orleans was to be Regent during the minority of the young King. His own unpopularity, however, and the remembrance of the ugly scandals which had been spread abroad concerning him, rendered the Regent's position one of no small difficulty and danger. But the times were not ripe for revolution yet, the wrongs of the people were to accumulate for three quarters of a century longer, and it was only at the close of the period just begun that the day of reckoning came. The force of the storm was to break upon the heads of the luckless but more innocent descendants of Monsieur and Madame, but its mutterings were already heard in the distance.[1]

The government of the Regent began under the most unfavorable conditions. The affairs of the kingdom were in a most deplorable

---

[1] Louis XVI. and Marie Antoinette *were* the descendants of Monsieur and Madame, although the Orleans family has never yet inherited the throne of France. (Louis Philippe was *elected* King on the expulsion of Charles X., and the heir to the crown at present is the young Duc d' Orleans, eight generations removed from Monsieur.) But Louis XVI. was the grandson of Louis XV., whose mother was Marie Adelaide, daughter of the Queen of Sardinia, who was Monsieur's daughter by his first marriage. Louis XVI. was, therefore, the great-great-grandson of Monsieur, while Marie Antoinette was the great-granddaughter of Madame as she was the daughter of Marie Therèse, who married Francis of Lorraine, the son of Charlotte Elizabeth, daughter of Monsieur and the second Madame.

state, and Louis XIV. had left an enormous amount of debt. He had also left a will in which he had given the young King into the charge of the Duc du Maine. This son of Madame de Montespan had always been a favorite of the King, who had before his death legitimized him and made him a prince of the blood. In making him the custodian of the young King, Louis is said to have himself felt that he had gone too far, and it was reported that he told the Duc du Maine that, while he could make this will in his favor, it would rest with himself to retain the position thus given him. It was also said that the King had, in a moment of irritation, confessed that he had made the will only because the Duc du Maine and Madame de Maintenon would give him no peace, but that he knew it would not stand.

This division of power could not but lead to dissension, and rendered the course of the Regent very difficult. His enemies were also those of his own household, for the Duc du Maine was the brother of his wife, and Madame d' Orleans had always favored his cause more than that of her husband; indeed, it was said that nothing would have pleased her better than to have seen her brother elevated to the highest position. This conduct on the part of Madame d' Orleans incensed Madame almost beyond endurance, but she wisely understood that it was useless to interfere with her daughter-in-law. She disapproved, moreover, of Madame d' Orleans' method of bringing up her children, and considered her the most indolent woman in the world, and quite unfitted for the position she occupied.

The Regent always treated his mother with the greatest respect, but he was wise enough to keep his own counsel about his affairs. St. Simon said that he merely talked to his mother of family matters, contemplated marriages, etc., or of such public acts as he was at liberty to speak. He never told her secrets, as he feared her discretion. For him, she had always exhibited the tenderest affection, but even her fondness could not always find excuses for his conduct, and sometimes, in her impatience, she was wont to say that it was time he should behave in a manner more befitting his years, as he was no longer a young man of twenty, but had reached the age of forty-two.

It is not pleasant to consider the character of the Regent. As Madame de Caylus said: "A singular and terrible brush is necessary to paint the portrait of Monsieur le Duc d' Orleans. Of all that we have seen of him and all that he was willing should be seen there was nothing real but the intelligence of which he really had much, that is to say, a quick comprehension, great penetration, much discernment, memory, and eloquence. Unfortunately, his character turned to evil, He had been made to believe that virtue was only a vain name, and that the world being made up of fools and people of intelligence, virtue and morality were the part of fools, and that people of wit affected only to have as much of them as suited their convenience."

It is difficult to do justice to this man, so overshadowed were his better qualities by the coarseness of his vice. He seems to have had no redeeming virtue unless the good nature with which he forgave his enemies could be so considered. But St. Simon declared that he carried this amiable inclination so far that it became a fault, and that it arose from a sort of insensibility and an innate timidity which caused him to fear his enemies so much that he treated them better than his friends. St. Simon, who seems to have been his most intimate friend, and who must have understood his character better than any one else, has given a very impartial and exhaustive study of it. Yet there were certain limitations in the mind of the writer which, in spite of the fact that he was genuinely fond of the subject, prevented him from doing full justice to some of the qualities of the Regent's understanding. In many respects he must have been in advance of his time. He had an active mind and was endowed with varied talents. A connoisseur of art, he had made a collection of paintings which, St. Simon said, rivalled those belonging to the Crown in number and value. He was also an amateur artist himself. He was fond of music, and composed two operas, and his ability in that direction was, according to Madame, recognized by musicians. Of the natural sciences he was an enthusiastic student, and was especially skilled in chemistry. It was his knowledge of this latter art which gave rise to the accusation of poisoning his relatives. Nothing, perhaps, could have been more unjust than these unwarranted fabrications, but they caused such unpleasant associations with the study that he gave it up. It was his habit, however, to become tired of everything. His mother said that she had always noticed that, while he was most eager to learn, no sooner had he mastered anything than it produced only ennui. St. Simon said that he was born bored, that never was a man so gifted with various talents or so skilled in methods of using them, while never was an existence so given over to weariness or so barren of results. He said that Madame explained her son's peculiarities by the fable that at his birth all the fairies who had been invited gave each a different talent, so that he possessed all, but that afterward came an old fairy whom they had all forgotten, who was so angry because she had not been invited that she cursed him with the inability to use any of the gifts of the others.

His fine natural endowment was spoiled by the abandonment with which he gave himself over to the gratification of his basest passions. One of his weaknesses was a fancied resemblance to Henry IV., but, unfortunately, he emulated only his vices. He had been thrown much upon his own resources in the days of his unpopularity, and had then amused himself by the exercise of his numerous talents; now, nothing pleased him but the wildest excesses.

The only excuses that can be offered for him are his having been so early forced into a distasteful marriage and his having, previously, been under the tutelage of the Abbé Dubois, who initiated his pupil in vice and instilled in him a disbelief in all virtue. This man was still the evil genius of the Regent. Madame could never endure him, for she had not forgotten that he had played a part in arranging the marriage of her son. But, as she said: "My son is like all his family, the things which they have been accustomed to in their youth must go in the ordinary way, that is why he can not separate himself from the Abbé Dubois of whose knavery he is well aware. That Abbé wanted to persuade me that the marriage of my son was very advantageous to him, I replied, 'Is there anything that will restore lost honor?' The Maintenon, also, made great promises to my son, but, thank God, she did not keep her word in any of them."

At another time she said of the Abbé: "The portrait of the Abbé Dubois is that of a fox lying in wait for a fowl." And again: "If the Abbé Dubois had died at his first lie, he would long ago have ceased to exist. . . . He is past-master of lying, above all where it is for his own advantage. If I should write all I know about that it would be a long litany."

In his youth Louis XIV. had, by no means, been an exemplar of morality, but in his old age and under the influence of Madame de Maintenon, he had surrounded himself with at least the semblance of piety and virtue. Now, all was changed, and the courtiers tried to appear worse than they really were, in order to find favor with their master. He was not deceived, however, and is said to have respected only, a man who was wholly depraved. For this reason his esteem for the Grand Prior amounted almost to veneration, for he, in addition to his other vices, had gone to bed drunk every night for forty years.

The Regent was not handsome even in the descriptions of his doting mother; although as may be supposed "he was not disagreeable" in her eyes, yet she wondered why he was so courted by women. He seems to have treated his favorites very cavalierly, bestowing his attentions upon several at the same time, and enjoying the jealousies engendered thereby.

He had grown fat and his face had become red as the result of his indulgence in eating and drinking, and he had an affection of the eyes which gave him always the appearance of squinting. He had already begun to exhibit symptoms of apoplexy and had several times alarmed his mother by the seizures which were the direct result of his excesses.

On September 24, 1715, Madame wrote from Paris: "My son I see but once a day, he stays with me only half an hour morning or evening. He eats at midday and at night with his wife. I eat alone, having a hundred people about me to whom I must talk whether I am cheerful or sad. The whole day people come who interrupt my writing, I must entertain them and that lasts until eight o'clock in the evening. In fact, I have here nothing but constraint and vexation and not the least joy or peace. So is my miserable life ordered, dear Louise. But one must give oneself up to the will of God. *Mein Gott*, dear Louise, I see well that you do not know this country. My son is lauded to the skies but all want to profit through him. There are fifty who ask for what one can have, and so forty-nine malcontents are created, and many enemies in all ranks. My son gives so much labor from six in the morning until midnight, that I fear he will become ill. Last Thursday he found himself so overheated, that he was bled sixteen ounces. Other days as on Friday, he held a council of finance eight hours, and worked afterward with different ministers until midnight. All is in such great disorder that it will take ten years to set matters right, and I fear that meanwhile my son will have a severe illness come upon him; this causes me great anxiety and trouble, neither do I see in the present or in the future anything but what is disagreeable to me.

"With this air and vexation, without the exercise to which I was so accustomed, it is not certain I will live the nine years my son has to rule, but life is agreeable only, when one can pass it in peace and quiet, whereas at other times it can but give torment. Be assured also, dear Louise, that when that little hour comes when our Lord God will take charge of me, I will quit this world without any regret."

St. Simon did not agree with Madame as to the pressing nature of the business of the Regent. While, at first, he may have been very closely occupied with affairs of State, he soon settled down into a mode of life in which his own pleasures and distractions were given a very prominent place. St. Simon thought he wasted a great deal of time also in giving audiences, many of which were unimportant and protracted too long. He allowed himself to be approached too easily, and by people who were likely to abuse the privilege. At five o'clock in the afternoon work was given up, and the evening was spent at the Luxembourg, at the opera, or in excursions to St. Cloud or other places in the country. At the suppers with which he finished the evenings no one was allowed to interrupt him, and however important the business it must be left until the next morning. By this time, however, he was in no condition to attend to business, for he and his guests soon drank themselves into a state of helpless intoxication. Even at dinners given at home, when Madame d'Orleans was induced to exert herself to entertain a little company, the guests were astonished, as St. Simon said, to see their host getting drunk at the beginning of the repast. At the little convivial gatherings, when the Regent invited a few choice spirits, greater freedom prevailed. The arrangements for the enjoyment of the pleasures of the table were very perfect. The cooking utensils were all of silver, and sometimes the Regent, as well as his guests, assisted in preparing the viands. Madame said that her son had learned the art of cooking in his Spanish campaigns. These orgies were kept up until a very late hour; but no matter how intoxicated the Regent became, he never revealed any secrets of his own or of the State. Madame was very much afraid that this dissipation would injure his health, but no remonstrance of hers or of his physicians would cause him to alter his course. He told his mother that, as he was tied down to work from morning until night, he must amuse himself a little afterward or he would die of melancholy.

Madame said of him once: "My son does not like the country at all, he likes nothing but the life of the city. It is with him as with Madame de Longueville, who was very much bored in Normandy where her husband was. Those around her said: '*Mon Dieu*, Madame, ennui is wearing you out, do you not want some amusement? There are dogs and beautiful forests, would you not like to hunt?'—'I do not like to hunt.'—'Would you not like to work?'—'No, I do not like work.'—'Would you like to walk, or to play at some game?'—'No, I do not care for the one or the other.' 'What would you have then?' they demanded of her. She replied, 'What shall I say?—I don't like innocent pleasures.'"

## CHAPTER IX.

### MADAME'S LIFE IN PARIS.

THE Regent found a companion and abettor in his eldest daughter, the Duchesse de Berri, and, unhappily, she rivalled her father in his worst faults. St. Simon said that at dinner it was customary for her to drink herself into a state of insensibility. In this vice, it is to be feared, she was not alone among the ladies of the Court, for Madame frequently commented on the habits of the ladies of rank in her time, both under the Regency and during the reign of Louis XIV., and intimated that the custom of drinking to excess was very common among them.

The Duchesse de Berri had made a great marriage, as she had been the wife of the younger brother of the Dauphin, grandson of Louis XIV. The Duc de Berri died, however, in 1714, and the Duchesse was left in freedom to live a very illy regulated life. Her historians expressed the greatest surprise that she was able to conceal her true character until after her marriage. But the young woman must have had extraordinary self-control, and, from motives of ambition, was able during the two years previous to her marriage to conduct herself in so exemplary a manner that there was no suspicion of the failings which afterward became so notorious. Madame de Caylus said that, even at the early age of twelve, thinking that she showed a tendency to become too fat, and fearing this might be an obstacle to the designs which were entertained for her, she resolved to eat hardly anything, to sleep little, and to take a great deal of exercise, although she was both lazy and a *gourmande*. As Madame de Caylus remarked;

"One cannot deny that a girl capable of forming such a resolution, at that age, from the sole motive of ambition and without being constrained by the authority of any one, might one day be very dangerous." Once married, she thought it of no use longer to deny herself, and showed her real tendencies. Two days after her marriage, she became intoxicated, with her father, at a supper which he gave to Madame la Dauphine, and in the presence of that Princess, Madame d' Orleans and the Duc de Berri. Not content with drinking at the table, she finished with liqueurs in a little cabinet, and Madame la Dauphine was very much ashamed of the condition in which she had to take her back to Versailles.

Madame was not inclined to be fond of her granddaughter, although her feelings seemed to be somewhat influenced by the conduct of the young Duchesse toward her. The latter inherited the intellectual qualities of her father, and, like him, could make herself very agreeable when she chose. At times Madame was pleased with her, and at others entirely out of patience at her conduct, and, indeed, others beside her virtuous grandmother were scandalized by her actions. Altogether, she seems to have been a shocking example of total depravity. Madame said that she had good capacity but had been badly brought up, and from her grandmother's statement of Madame d' Orleans's methods, one may well imagine it.

The second daughter had tastes quite different from her sister, and finding herself in an uncongenial atmosphere at home, wished to enter a convent. This idea was favored by her mother, but bitterly opposed by Madame who wrote; " Madame d' Orleans is not of my mind in regard to her daughters. She wishes they might all become nuns. She is not stupid enough to think that will take them to heaven; it is on her part pure laziness, because she is the most indolent woman in the world, and fears if she keeps them with her she will have the trouble of bringing them up." Madame deplored the mode of life now adopted by the royal family, for, as she said, there was no longer any court life, as there was in Germany or in France in the time of Monsieur. Now, they no longer dined together and did not meet in the great apartments in the evening. Madame d' Orleans would not make the least exertion and remained always lying on a couch, while Madame de Berri at Luxembourg followed the example of her mother, so there could be no court.

On November 27, 1717, Madame wrote from St. Cloud: "St. Cloud is only a summer residence. Many of my people have rooms without chimneys; they can not, therefore, pass the winter here. I would be the cause of their death, and I am not hard enough for that; those who suffer always inspire me with pity. If it depended only on myself, I would rather remain here for the winter, than return to the Palais Royal where I have not room enough. I have but one warm room and a closet. But it is neccessary to conform to custom, and I have all my life taken the part which was most reasonable, rather than that which was most agreeable. I neither fear nor avoid the heat or cold. My son is like me, he loves warm weather. The heat must be very great when we complain of it, or perspire. My taste leads me to see little company, and a crowd causes more repugnance than pleasure. I like better to be alone than to have to worry myself to find something to say to everybody, because the French take it amiss if you do not talk to them and they become malcontents. So I must trouble myself to talk to them. I am, therefore, content and tranquil when they leave me in my solitude. I do not like to make visits, and hate ceremonies and all that partakes of them. As soon as I have had a moment free, I have been in the chapel praying for my son, whose eye is a little better. He had not been able to distinguish colors, and when I was with him Cardinal Polignac came to see him, and my son discerned the color of his red robe very well. There is then a sensible improvement. While he has been under treatment, he has refrained from excess in drinking and eating and all kinds of misconduct, but I fear that after his cure, he will return to his ordinary life."

The Regent suffered from an affection of one of his eyes, which, according to his mother's account, was the result of being struck by a tennis ball when a child. Another historian, however, said that the blow, which, as it happened, was only too well deserved, came from a lady's fan. Madame was much concerned for fear her son would eventually become blind, as he soon relapsed into his dissipations, causing an access of the malady.

From Paris, Madame wrote on January 13, 1718: "The late storms have done great damage in Holland and Friesland, three villages have been flooded, and twenty thousand persons have perished; this is frightful. I am very much troubled at what is going on at St. James, and fear that things are going from bad to worse. No one shall know what you write to me on this subject. The English are a bad race; and since the time of King William they are more spoiled, and have fallen into great vices. Some one has said that islanders are more false and wicked than the inhabitants of *terra firma*. One had never more need of the grace of God, because this is a terrible epoch of ours. One hears of nothing but quarrels and strife, of thefts, murders, and all kinds of vice. That old serpent the Devil has been delivered from his chains and reigns in the air. Good Christians must devote themselves to prayer."

Madame was expecting a visit from her daughter, but could not believe that she would get there by the 10th of February as was expected, for, as she said, a long experience had taught her that the things which people most desire in this world are those which frequently turn out as badly as possible. February 20, 1718, she wrote from Paris: "My children of Lorraine have arrived. My daughter is beside herself with joy. I do not find her much changed, but her husband is horribly so. He had, formerly, a fine color, but now he is of a red brown tint. He is larger than my son. I can say that my children are as fat as myself. My daughter is gay and content, but her husband is preoccupied. Yesterday she had a high fever, God grant that it may not be the forerunner of the small-pox, because neither the Duc de Lorraine nor my son has had it, and the Duc would not be kept from his wife. Three of his brothers have died already of that frightful malady. I am therefore uneasy on this account. I will write you on Wednesday how it is."

In spite of Madame's fears all went well during the visit, and although it lasted about a month, the time of departure came all too soon. On the 10th of March, Madame wrote: "My children of Lorraine will leave in three days; I have a full heart; my daughter would like to stay longer but the Duc wishes to return. My daughter, thank God, is so well established in her good principles, that she can mix in any society without being spoiled, but never has anything been seen like the young people now-a-days, it makes one's hair stand on end. In short, one sees and hears only the most horrible things. My daughter said that, although I had written them to her, she had not believed them until she had them every day under her eyes. The young people believe no longer in God, and forget all exercises of piety, and God abandons them. It is sad to live in a time like this, when honest people have such surroundings, it causes universal disgust. Thank God that my daughter knows still what is virtue, and that she is inspired with a just horror of the life they lead here. That is a great consolation for me." The Duchesse de Lorraine seems to have been of a placid, contented, disposition. Madame wondered how she could love her husband so much, and why she was not jealous, for, although he was openly unfaithful to her, she went on her way as if seeing nothing, happy if ever he showed her a little of the affection which had been diverted to another.

Madame said, afterward, that her daughter did not remain long enough for her good influence to produce any effect where it was so much needed, but she repeated with pardonable pride that people had asked her how she had managed to bring her up so well. One cannot begrudge the satisfaction she took in this one good child. Possibly the Regent might have been better, if his mother had had more to do with his bringing up. Although a fond mother she did not lack firmness. Of this she wrote once: "The late Monsieur made my children fear me, because he always menaced them with my severity. He had not, otherwise a mind to trouble himself much. He loved his children so much that he could not scold them, and always came to me with complaints. I would say: 'But, Monsieur, are not the children yours as well as mine?' He would reply: 'I do not know how to scold them. They do not fear me. They only fear you.'" If it was true, as had been said, that Elizabeth had been glad to escape the severe rule of her mother, this visit, after so long an absence, appeared to give both unalloyed pleasure. Her mother said: "My daughter is ugly; she was less so formerly because she had a fine skin, but now she is all burned by the sun, that changes her and makes her appear old. She has an ugly, turned-up nose, her eyes are hollow, but her figure is well preserved, and she dances well, and besides has good manners, one can well see who she is. I know people who pride themselves on their good manners, who are very far from being as well bred as she. Such as she is I am well content, and I like it better that she is virtuous than that she should be pretty and coquettish like the others."

The King, who owed the Duc de Lorraine a good deal of money, paid him a hundred thousand francs, which went towards defraying the expenses of this journey. Madame said that this little trip cost him the sum of a hundred thousand *écus*.

The relatives gave the Duchesse de Lorraine very handsome presents. The Duchesse de Berri gave a chest of drawers decorated with gilded ornaments and filled with all sorts of stuffs, scarfs, coiffures, etc., all in the latest mode, and the Regent gave his sister a little case in which were enclosed all the articles necessary for serving tea, coffee, or chocolate, with cups in white porcelain decorated with gold and enamels.

## CHAPTER X.

### THE ROYAL HOUSEHOLD.

OF the manner in which life went on for her, Madame gave an account in a letter written from St. Cloud, May 19, 1718: "I went to Paris yesterday, to see my son and his family, and to see the representation of a new piece in which there is nothing very extraordinary although there are two fine bits. It is called *Artaxarte*. Just as I entered the box they gave me your letter of the 7th. I am well at St. Cloud where I am quiet, while at Paris they do not leave me a moment in peace. One hands me a petition, the other asks that I shall interest myself for him, another wishes an audience, another wants an answer to the letters he has written. One cannot stand it. They seem to be astonished that I am not charmed with that sort of thing. In this world the great have their troubles as well as the small. That is not surprising, but what makes it more trying for the first is that they are always surrounded by a crowd which prevents them from concealing their chagrin and from retiring into solitude. They are always on exhibition."

On the 9th of June she wrote as follows: "I returned from Paris last night at ten o'clock where I had been from eleven o'clock in the morning assisting at a long and tiresome ceremony in the Convent they call the *Abbaye-aux-Bois*. They were going to lay the first corner-stone in a church they are to build. They came to meet me with drums, fifes, and trumpets, and we had to go through a long street. I really lost countenance. You can imagine what a crowd gathered. After the Mass when they had very good music, we went to the place where they were digging the foundations.

"The priest chanted psalms and recited, in Latin, prayers of which I did not comprehend a word. I was seated in an arm-chair upon a platform in a place covered with a carpet. When I was seated, they brought me a stone upon which was engraved my name, and in the middle was my medal. They threw on the mortar with which I was all bespattered, then they placed upon it another stone upon which I was to give my benediction. I confess, the idea made me laugh. I sent the first gentleman of my household, M. de Montague, to place the stone, for I could not mount and descend the ladders. This ceremony lasted an hour and a half. There was afterward a great deal of music, and the whole terminated by a *Te Deum*.

I afterward went to the Palais Royal. It was horribly warm. I dined with my son and three of his daughters. Then I went to the Luxembourg to see Madame de Berri. I was so tired that when I found myself in an airy apartment I went to sleep like a marmot. I was very much ashamed, but the thing was done. At five o'clock I returned to the Palais Royal and was with Madame d' Orleans at the play to see a new actor who made his debut. He played Orestes in *Andromache*. My son rejoined us at the fourth act. For an afterpiece they gave the *Vendanges de Suresne*. This would have been an amusing comedy if one had not seen it a hundred times. The heat was so great that I almost melted."

At another time Madame gave an account of a visit to a Jesuit college, at some distance from the Palais Royal, where the scholars were to play a piece called *Le Point d' Honneur*. She said: "The children played very well. My little cousin La Tremouille had a part in which he acquitted himself marvellously well. But the affair had to end badly for me. They had placed my arm-chair upon the platform, and when I started to go away I forgot the steps by which it was necessary to descend, made a false step, and fell. They made haste to pick me up as you may imagine, and I did not hurt myself at all, only the glass in one of my watches was broken. I laughed when I got back to the Palais Royal, and I laugh yet whenever I think of the gravity with which two great Jesuits came to pick me up. It would have made a picture. When I came back to the Palais Royal, it was six o'clock. I was at the play with my son, his wife, and the people who were in my carriage. They gave *Ariane* and the *Sicilian*. At a quarter of ten, I got into the carriage again to come back here, but at the Tuileries we were stopped, for the fine weather had caused so many people to promenade in the garden that there was a multitude of carriages before the gates, the passage was blocked up, and it was after ten before we were liberated. It was not until half-past twelve that I got to bed."

Madame was not long, however, so free from care that she could give herself up to the enjoyment of plays and ceremonies.

The many enemies of the Regent, headed by his brother-in-law the Duc de Maine, were always exciting some disturbance. On the 24th of June she wrote: "I am very much upset to-day because the enemies of my son have excited all the Parliament against him. He has a great many enemies, and above all the people to whom he has done the most good. One could not believe how ungrateful this nation is. The result of this must be revolution and civil war. May God preserve us from that. You may well see, my dear Louise, why I should have so much uneasiness. I cannot talk a long time with you this morning for I must go to the church (it is a great feast day), and I dare not say what I think by post."

On the 25th of August she wrote again from St. Cloud: "The Parliament annoys my son and excites the *bourgeoisie* and the people of Paris against him more than ever. It can only result in great calamities. Every night on going to bed, I thank God that no misfortune has arrived during the day. Many people would like to have the King of Spain[1] as king here. That is a feeble personage who would let himself be led more easily than my son. Each one dreams but of his own interest. They pretend that the King of Spain has a genuine right to the throne of France; that a wrong was done him when they made him renounce his country. That is agitated in considering the possibility of the death of the little King. If he should die, my son would be King, but he would not be in greater security than he is at present, and that death would be a great misfortune for him.

"I have never seen a summer like this. It has not rained for three weeks and the heat grows greater every day. The leaves on the trees are as dry as if a fire had passed over them. There are prophecies that it will

[1] The King of Spain, formerly known as the Duc d'Anjou, was the grandson of Louis XIV. and the uncle of Louis XV. In accepting the throne of Spain he had renounced all right to the succession in France.

rain on Wednesday. God grant it, but until it does rain they will not see me in Paris. We find it very warm here, but all who come from Paris say 'How cool St. Cloud is.' Paris is a horrible place, very hot and vile-smelling."

At length affairs reached a crisis and the Regent took the initiative. On the 30th of August Madame wrote: "If my son had delayed twenty-four hours, the Parliament had formed a fine project, to make the Duc du Maine King of France in declaring the majority of the King and giving the Duc direction of all his affairs. My son has disconcerted them. He has taken the Duc du Maine away from the King and degraded him from his rank. They say the Premier President was so frightened that he was petrified as if he had seen the head of Medusa. But Medusa herself could not have been more furious than the Duchesse du Maine. She has been heard to say that she will find means to give the Regent a stroke that will make him bite the dust."

On October 15, 1718, Madame wrote: "My son is not in safety and that troubles me extremely. I try my best to be resigned to the Divine will and to accept all that it sends, but the heart of a mother is too tender in regard to her only son. One could be better prepared for lions, tigers, and all kinds of ferocious beasts, than for bad people, especially when ambition and cupidity are the cause of their animosity. The people who criticise do not know the deplorable state in which my son found the kingdom. When a change came, each one imagined that he was going to become rich. They praise him who governs and look for him to do wonders, but when their hopes are not realized because they are impossible, then praise is changed to blame. It would not be so bad if these complaints spent themselves in words only, but the malcontents form intrigues and plots. The French restrain themselves in nothing and do not know what gratitude is."

The time came for decisive action, and the

Regent arrested the Duc and Duchesse du Maine and imprisoned them. Madame wrote that Madame d'Orleans could not be made to believe that her brother had been guilty of conspiracy, but said that since her husband had adopted such measures he must have good reasons. Madame d'Orleans blamed her sister-in-law the Duchesse for the difficulty, while the Princesse de Condé, mother of the Duchesse, believed all the fault to rest with the Duc du Maine. Madame du Maine was acknowledged to have much wit and intelligence, and, as Madame said, "was lord and master of her husband." Madame was very much alarmed for the safety of her son, and considered it very rash for him to drive about at night as he persisted in doing. On February 25, 1719, she wrote as follows: "I talked yesterday with my son, and wanted to know if it was true that his wife had advised him to go out at night, and to go to the masked ball. He acknowledged it and added that Madame de Berri had said that I wanted to be the only one to govern him, and that he would injure his reputation if he showed any fear of his life. Tell me that there is any devil in hell worse than that woman. She begins to walk well in the footsteps of her mother. You can well comprehend how my anguish grows when I see that my son finds in his wife neither comfort nor safety. It is a satisfaction to me that I have always regarded this marriage as a scourge, but it is very painful to have before my eyes every day that wicked woman. She cannot even endure her children to have any affection for me."

Shortly afterwards Madame wrote: "Lord Stairs troubled me very much yesterday, for he said that there had been a rumor in England that my son had been assassinated; that proves that the party which has been formed against him has always in mind the idea of assassinating him, and spreads the news in advance to see how it will be received and what effect it will produce. I learned also that the Duchesse de Berri gave a supper to her father in a house near Versailles, and they did not come away until three o'clock in the morning. Over and above the danger that results for the life of my son, that does the greatest wrong to his honor and reputation. But it is better to speak of other things, because the more I think of it the more sad and irritated I become. In France,, nothing can pass quietly, the princes are so unhappy as not to be able to take one step without having everybody aware of it. Their servants are their most formidable enemies." As usual, Madame suspected her old enemy, Madame de Maintenon, of complicity in the plots of the Duc du Maine, and charged her and the Princesse des Ursins with inciting the Duc and his wife to intrigue. She said; "The affair of the Duc du Maine is not one of the things that one can forget, at least while those two old wretches are in life, because they incite the Duc du Maine, and his little devil of a wife concocts all sorts of things against my son. Madame des Ursins has at least that much good that she does not seek to bring the good God into her schemes."

But Madame's *bête noire* was soon to be removed. Madame de Maintenon had become a very old woman. In February, 1719, Madame wrote: "I made my son laugh day before yesterday. I asked him how Madame de Maintenon was. He replied; 'Wonderfully well.' I said to him; 'How can she be, at her age?' He said: 'Don't you know that the good God, to punish the Devil, makes him dwell a long time in so bad a body.'"

In a letter written on the 18th of April, 1719, Madame announced the death of Madame de Maintenon, which event had occurred on the Saturday before between four and five o'clock in the afternoon. The manner of the announcement, while shocking to one's sense of propriety, was perfectly characteristic. Madame was a vigorous hater, and she had too little regard for conventionalities to try to hide her real feelings upon the occasion. Madame de Maintenon had reached the age of eighty-six, which Madame charged her with having reduced by four years in her own statements, yet she died from the effects of an attack of measles. Madame attributed her illness to the anger and disappointment caused by the arrest of the Duc du Maine, and said that the loss of the hope of sharing his longed-for power had prevented her from enjoying a moment's rest or contentment since. She wrote to Herr Von Harling : "Saturday evening we lost a pious soul at St. Cyr, the old Maintenon. . . . If she had died twenty years sooner I would have rejoiced heartily, but now it gives me neither pleasure nor pain. . . . In the other world, where all is equal and there is no difference of rank, they can decide whether she will remain with the King or with her first husband, the paralytic Scarron, and if the King knew all that had been concealed from him he would without doubt willingly give her to Scarron."

About this time the Duchesse de Berri fell ill, and her grandmother wrote of her condition, to the Countess Louise, as follows. "The Duchesse de Berri is ill, she has a fever and is depressed. It is the effect of the horribly strong perfumes that she always has in her apartments, and which do her harm. I have warned her of it but she would not listen to me. It is, besides, impossible to be well with her frightful gluttony. Every evening she sits down to the table at eight or nine o'clock and eats until three in the morning. If anything should happen, my son would be inconsolable, for there is no one in the world he loves better."

Her illness continued and on the 17th of July, 1719, Madame wrote: "The Duchesse de Berri died to-night between two and three o'clock. Her end was very easy, they said she died just as if she were going to sleep. My son remained with her until she lost consciousness. She was his favorite child."

In a letter written three days later, Madame said: "They were so much embarrassed as to her funeral oration, that they judged it better not to make any at all. She said that she died without regret since she was reconciled to God, and that if she lived longer, she would be likely to offend again. That touched us more than I can express. She was really a good person, and if her mother had taken more pains and had brought her up better, one would have had more good to say. I acknowledge that her loss goes to my heart. But let us talk of other things. That you could not read part of my last letter is because at the moment I ended it one of my dogs seized it and destroyed a part of it. I see that you do not love dogs, because if you loved them as I do, you would overlook these little defects. I have a little dog called *Reine inconnue*, that comprehends as well as any person, and whenever I leave it weeps and howls as soon as it sees me no longer.

"When I first came to France, I wanted to walk in the garden at Versailles one night. The Swiss, who was on guard, refused to let me pass; I said to him: 'My good Swiss, let me pass, I am the wife of the brother of the King.' 'Has the King a brother?' he replied. I answered: 'How is it that you do not know, how long have you served the

King? '—' For thirty years.'—' You should know that the King has a brother, for every time he passes, you present arms.'—' Yes,' responded the Swiss, ' when they beat the drum, I present arms, but I have never been told why, and if the King has a brother, or children, it is all the same to me.' I made the King laugh when I repeated this dialogue to him."

Later, Madame wrote: "As to the death of the poor Duchesse de Berri, I know well who is to blame for this misfortune; it is that wicked Mouchy, the favorite of the poor Duchesse, who has caused her death; she killed her as surely as if she had plunged a knife into her throat; the Duchesse was consumed by a slow fever; her favorite brought her all sorts of things to eat in the night, *fricassées*, little *pâtés*, melons, salad, milk, prunes, figs; she gave her iced beer to drink. During fourteen days she had not wanted any physician to come, the fever had been increasing and the invalid was not able to stand it."

The Duchesse left an enormous amount of debts which her father had to pay. The estate of her husband, which she had enjoyed during her life, went back to the Crown, together with her pension. Her affairs were left in the greatest disorder, and she had probably been pillaged frightfully by her favorites, but Madame said the wages of her servants had not been paid for two or three years. She also wrote: "All the people in the service of the Duchesse seem entirely consoled for her loss, I also am consoled; because of a good many things I have learned since her death, and which it is impossible to write." According to Madame's statement the legacy of the Duchesse to her father was four hundred thousand pounds of debts.

The sister of Madame de Berri carried out her intention of becoming a nun. The arrangement made in regard to the matter is referred to in a letter written from Paris, April 22, 1719: "I read this morning my dozen chapters in the Bible, the 37th, 38th,

39th, and 40th Psalms, the first four of Ecclesiastes, the 22d, 23d, and 24th of St. Luke, and the 4th of St. John. I am going to talk with you for half an hour and afterward will go to the convent of Val de Grâce where my granddaughter is to arrive in coming from Chelles, which she has just left while the present abbess retires and renders her account to the nuns. They have given her a pension of twelve thousand francs until she finds another abbey vacant to which she can be transferred. I do not believe there is another abbess as young as my granddaughter. She will be twenty-one next August. Monday, I went to the Prince of Conti, who invited me to come to his Château de Choisy, two hours from here. It is a beautiful residence that the Grande Mademoiselle built, and which she left to M. le Dauphin, but the King found it too far from Versailles, and wished that the Dauphin would change it for Meudon which belonged to Madame Louvois, whose heirs have sold Choisy to the Prince de Conti. It is a very agreeable place situated along the Seine, the gardens are so near the water that one can have the pleasure of fishing. Wednesday being my great day for correspondence, I will not go to take leave of the King and to attend the play. Thursday morning I will return to Paris. I will write you a line and after having been at the church, I will leave at mid-day for my dear St. Cloud, where, God permitting, I will pass the summer. You know now all my plans."

The investiture of the new abbess took place in September and was described by Madame in the following letter to the Countess Louise: "I promised to tell you about my trip to Chelles. I went away Thursday at seven o'clock with the Duchesse de Brancas, Madame de Chasteautier, and Madame Von Rathsamhausen. We arrived at half-past ten. My grandson, the Duc de Chartres, had already arrived, my son came a quarter of an hour afterward, and then Mademoiselle de Valois; Madame d'Orleans had herself bled expressly so as not to go. She and the abbess are not very good friends, and besides her excessive laziness would have prevented her putting herself out and getting up so early. We went to the church, the *prie-dieu* of the abbess being placed in the choir of the nuns; it was in violet velvet, covered with golden *fleur-de-lis*. My *prie-dieu* was against the balustrade. My son and his daughter were behind my chair, because the Princes of the blood cannot kneel upon my rug. This is a right reserved to the grandsons of France. All the musicians of the King were in the gallery; Cardinal Noailles said Mass. The altar was very fine,—it is made of black and white marble with four great columns of black marble; there are four beautiful statues of white marble representing holy abbesses. One resembles our abbess so strongly that one might believe it her portrait. It was, however, done before my granddaughter was born, as she is only twenty-one. A dozen monks of the order, clothed in superb chasubles, came to serve the Mass and brought out the abbess; she came with a very good air followed by two abbesses and a half dozen nuns of her convent. She made a deep reverence to the altar and to me, and kneeled before the Cardinal, who was seated in a great armchair before the altar. They brought in state the Confession of Faith, which she read, and after the Cardinal had recited some prayers, he gave her a book which contained the rules of the convent. She then came back to her place, and after they had read the *Credo* and the *Offertory*, she came with the offering accompanied by the abbess and her nuns; they brought for offering two great candles, and two loaves of bread, one of which was gilded and the other silvered. After the Cardinal had received the Sacrament, she came and kneeled before him and gave him the cross; he re-conducted her to her seat, not to her *prie-dieu*, but to her abbess's seat which was a kind of throne, placed upon the dais of a Princess of the blood, with the *fleur-de-lis*. As soon as she was seated the trumpets and haut-boys were heard, and the Cardinal, followed by all his priests, placed himself near the altar on the left hand, and they chanted the *Te Deum.* All the nuns came forward two and two, to testify their submission to their abbess, in making a deep reverence to her; that made one think of the honors they render to Athys when they make him high priest of Cybèle, as they come also two and two to salute him. I thought they were going to chant as in the opera.

> "*Que devant vous, tout s'abaisse et tout tremble.*
> *Vive heureux, vos jours sont nostre Espoir ;*
> *Rien n'est si beau que de voir ensemble.*
> *Un grand merite avec un grand pouvoir*
> *Que l'on benisse*
> *Le Ciel propisse*
> *Qui dans vos mains*
> *Met les sort des humains.*

"After the *Te Deum* we entered the convent, and at half-past twelve we sat down to the table, my son, my grandson, the Duc de Chartres; the Princesse Victoire; the young demoiselle d' Auvergne, daughter of the Duc d' Albret, and three ladies who were with me. The Abbess placed herself in her position in the refectory, at a table of forty covers, with her sister, Mademoiselle de Valois, the two ladies who accompanied her, a dozen abbesses, and all the other nuns of the convent. It was droll to see all these black robes around the table. The servants of my son served a very fine repast; they let the people carry away the *confitures* after the dinner was finished. At a quarter to five my carriage came and we returned here."

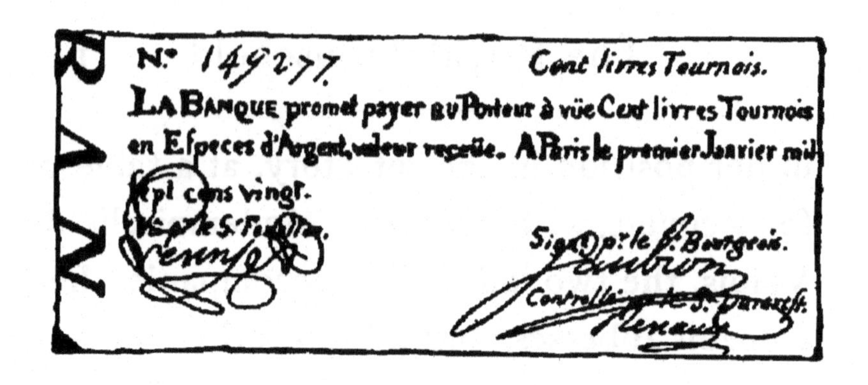
N° 149277 Cent livres Tournois.
LA BANQUE promet payer au Porteur à vüe Cent livres Tournois en Especes d'Argent, valeur reçeüe. A Paris le premier Janvier mil sept cens vingt.
Vû p. le S. Fenellon.
Signé p. le S. Bourgeois.
Controllé p. le S. Durevest.

# CHAPTER XI.

## THE MISSISSIPPI BUBBLE.

IN the autumn of 1719, the Mississippi Bubble was at its period of fullest expansion. Madame believed in the integrity of Law and was, naturally, pleased with the financier who was assisting the Regent to rid himself of his debts. The easy state of the money market, also, produced an agreeable change in her own affairs, for the Regent augmented her pension. Heretofore she had always complained that it was difficult for her to keep up her large household and live according to her rank, and that even without entering into any unnecessary expenses it was as much as she could do to make both ends meet. She did not entertain, and was unable to travel even when her health required it, for she was not permitted to travel incognito, and it was too expensive to do it according to her station. Now, also, that the Duchesse de Berri had died and left so rich an inheritance to the King, the Regent felt that he could add to his mother's income without rendering it possible for people to say that he enriched his family at the expense of the King.

Money was plentiful, prices became very high, but people were becoming rich so fast that they vied with each other in lavishness of expenditure. Many curious stories of the time were told. In one of her letters, Madame said: "The story of the coachman of M. Law is very true. He presented two coachmen to his master, who asked if they were good. The man replied: 'They are so good, that I will keep the one you do not take, for myself.' They tell a hundred other stories of the same kind. There is nothing talked of but M. Law's bank. One lady who could not get to see him tried a singular method of getting an opportunity to talk to him. She gave orders to her coachman to upset her before Law's door. He ran out on hearing her screams, thinking she must have broken her neck, but she hastened to tell him it was only a stratagem in order to see him. Another lady named Madame de Bouchu invented another method. She had spies who told her what Monsieur Law did, and having learned that he was to dine with Madame de Simiane, one of the ladies of honor to the Duchesse d'Orleans, she had people to cry fire during the repast. All the guests ran from the table. M. Law having also come down to see where the fire was, this Madame de Bouchu sprang upon him, so to speak, and said it was a ruse on her part in order to get an opportunity to ask him for shares."

Another story related by Madame is that of Dr. Chirac, who was one day called to see a lady who was ill. "While he was in the ante-chamber, some one said that the shares had fallen very much. The Doctor, who had many shares in the Mississippi, was impressed by the news, and while sitting by her and feeling her pulse, said to himself, 'It is lower, it is lower, it is lower.' Hearing him speak thus, the invalid screamed, her servants ran to her. She said: 'I am going to die; M. Chirac has just said, for the third time, that my pulse is going down.' The Doctor came to himself and said: 'You are dreaming, your pulse beats wonderfully well. I was thinking of the shares of the Mississippi on which I am going to lose as they go down.'" Madame comprehended nothing of finance and grew very tired of the talk of shares and millions. She was very much out of patience, also, with the conduct of some people of rank, and thought it a most ignoble thing that Princesses of the blood should go to the bank and should join in the mad quest of gold. In a letter written January 27, 1720, she said: "Three dukes belonging to the first families have, according to my opinion, done most unworthy things: the Duc d'Autin, who is a son of the Montespan and, consequently brother of my daughter-in-law and Madame la Duchesse; the Duc Maréchal d'Estrees, and the Duc de la Force; the first has bought all the stuffs to sell them higher, the second all the coffee and chocolate, the third has done worse, for he has bought all the candles and sold them at auction. The other day, as he came out of the opera, the young people followed him chanting the chorus of the opera of *Phaeton*:

> '*Allez, allez, répandre la lumière,*
> *Puisse un heureux destin vous conduire à la fin*
> *De votre brilliante carrière.*
> *Allez, allez, répandre la lumière.*'

You can imagine how every one laughed."

Madame bewailed the lack of gold. There was nothing now but notes, and she had always been used to carry gold pieces in her pocket. At last this lack of coin became a serious embarrassment. People began to distrust the notes and demanded coin in payment for supplies, and her steward did not have it. Matters were nearing a crisis. On July 18, 1720, Madame wrote as follows: "Before replying to your good letter, I must tell you, my dear Louise, what a horrible fright I had yesterday. I went in a carriage, as usual, to the Carmelites, and there I found Madame de Lude. We were very quiet when Madame de Chasteautier arrived, pale as death, and said to me: 'Madame, one cannot conceal what has happened from you; you will find all the courts of the Palais Royal filled with people; they have carried out people from the bank who have been crushed to death. Law has been obliged to save himself in the Palais Royal; they have broken his carriage into a thousand pieces and have broken down the gates.' You can imagine the impression made upon me by such news; I would not show it, however, for in such a case one must not lack resolution. I caused myself to be conducted to the King as usual. There was such a crush in the rue St. Honoré that I could not pass for half an hour. I heard the people inveigh against Law, but they said nothing about my son and they addressed benedictions to me. I arrived at last at the Palace, but all was quiet there and the people had gone away. My son came to see me and assured me that all this tumult was caused by some drunken fellows. The people who had been suffocated were not driven to demand payment of their notes by great distress; one of them had a hundred crowns in his pocket, and none of those arrested were without money. The invasion of the Palais Royal was the work of some malcontents who have a mortal hatred of my son."

On September 5, 1720, she wrote: "They are quiet here, but there is much murmuring and in a moment serious disorders may occur. Some days ago the lackeys permitted themselves a great insolence. I cannot understand how such excesses are tolerated; they overwhelmed the daughter of M. Law, a poor child returning from school, with insults, and threw stones at her. I see well what is the cause of these disorders: the young people now-a-days mix with their lackeys too much, they have them for accomplices in all sorts of infamies, the lackeys imitate their masters, and so these gentlemen cannot complain. The Queen of Prussia has told me of the explosion of the powder magazine, but she did not tell me whether she was frightened; the fact is, that all the windows of the Château were broken. That makes me think of an adventure that happened to Madame de Durfurt, who was my lady of the bed-chamber. She was the sister of the Maréchal de Duras, who was Governor of Besançon, and at the house of her brother there was a garden decorated with statues, among which was one representing Jupiter, which was so beautiful that the King bought it, and it is now at Versailles. Madame de Durfurt, finding herself alone in the garden of her brother one day, stopped a moment before this statue and said to it: 'Now, Monsieur Jupiter, they say you used to talk; we are alone, speak to me then, as you seem about to open your mouth.' At the moment she finished speaking, a powder-mill exploded with a frightful noise; Madame de Durfurt thought it was Jupiter who answered. She was so frightened that she fell fainting to the ground and had to be carried out of the garden."

The next day, Madame wrote from St. Cloud: "For the last eight days I have received many letters in which they threaten to burn me at St. Cloud and to burn my son at the Palais Royal. My son has not said a word to me of what passes here; he follows the example of his father who used to say: 'All is well, provided Madame does not know it.'" On the 20th she wrote again: "Three days ago, I received an anonymous letter which made me laugh heartily; they advised me to shut my son up as a lunatic, as a means of saving his life. My son has already slept many times in the Tuileries. I fear, however, that the King cannot get used to him, because my son has never been able to play with children. He does not like them."

The Mississippi Bubble had burst. Law was obliged to fly, and took refuge at one of his estates, leaving the Regent to bear the brunt of the unfortunate financial situation. Madame did not pretend to pass judgment upon the cause of all this misfortune, for as she said, she could not comprehend his system at all, and could not believe that he had intended to defraud the people.

## CHAPTER XII.

### THE END.

LIFE with the royal family went on afterward in the same *bourgeois* manner, as Madame styled it. Little as she had cared for the ceremonies of court life, she was annoyed by the absence of the forms to which she had been accustomed. In the palmy days of the late King, that royal personage had been the centre of an assemblage which represented the pomp and circumstance of a court in a way that has never been equalled. Now all was in confusion. As Madame said: "In the royal family all the relations hate each other like the Devil. The two sisters, that is to say, Madame la Duchesse and the wife of my son, are far from loving each other and mutually hold each other capable of bad designs. The legitimate princes of the blood cannot endure that the illegitimate should be placed on terms of equality with them. Madame la Duchesse declares herself for her sons against her brother, the Duc du Maine, while Madame d'Orleans, on the contrary, has taken the part of her brother against the princes of the blood; that, as you may believe, has caused a terrible hatred which, in my opinion, will last during their whole lives. Although M. le Duc and the Prince de Conti are doubly brothers-in-law, since each married the sister of the other, they detest each other so much that it is really scandalous. My son has done all sorts of kindnesses to the princes of the blood; he has augmented their pensions, but they have no gratitude toward him; on the contrary, they hate him to the death; they are false and wicked people. The Prince de Conti is thought to be a little deranged; he is full of caprices and reason has no control over him; sometimes he tells his wife that he wants to kill her and sometimes he takes so strong a friendship for her that he will not let her go away a step. Once he came to find his wife after she had gone to bed, with a loaded pistol in his hand, and said to her that she should not escape him, he was going to blow her brains out. As she knew his manias, she also had pistols under her pillow, and seizing one, said: 'Take care not to miss me, for if you do not kill me instantly you are dead. Draw first.' That was a woman very courageous and resolute. The Prince, who is not very brave, as he showed himself in the last campaign, was afraid and retired."

At another time, Madame wrote: "There is no longer any court in France and it is the fault of the Maintenon, who seeing that the King did not wish to proclaim her Queen, did not wish to have any more receptions and persuaded the Dauphine to remain in her room, where there was no distinction of rank or dignity. Under the pretext that it was only in play, the old one led the young Dauphine and the Princesses to serve her at her toilette and table, she persuaded them to present the dishes, to change the plates, to pour what she drank. Everthing was upside down and nobody knew what was her place or what she was. I never was mixed up in all that; but when I went to see the lady, I placed myself near her niche in an arm-chair and never served at the table or her toilette. Some people advised me to do as the Dauphine and the Princesses. I replied: 'I have never been brought up to do mean things, and I am too old to give myself up to child's play.' After that they did not speak of it again."

Madame blamed the Duchesse d'Orleans for permitting the ladies to present themselves to her in loose robes and flying draperies, and thought it shocking that her granddaughters were allowed to go about without the bodices of their gowns in the morning. The young ladies remained in this undress costume sometimes as late as one o'clock, and once when Madame dined with them, one of them did not appear until the second course, because the body of her dress could not be found, and she did not dare to appear before her grandmother without it. Madame wrote in 1720: "I do not hold a court any more, because it is very rarely that the *dames à tabouret* come to me, as they cannot make up their minds to wear any but loose robes. I have invited them as usual, to assist at the audience that I was to give to the Ambassadors from Malta, but not one of them came. When the late King and Monsieur lived, they were very glad to come to my audiences. They were not then accustomed to court dress, and when they did not come dressed enough Monsieur threatened to speak to the King."

Of the fashions of the time, Madame said: "I am far behind the modes, I put them all aside, such as the paniers, which I do not wear, and the flying robes which I cannot endure and will not admit into my presence, it seems to me an indecency, they have the air as if one was just getting out of bed. There is no rule for the fashions, the dress-makers and the hair dressers invent them to their taste. I have never followed the extreme mode of high coiffures."

On March 8, 1721, Madame wrote: "My son gets along very well with me, he professes much friendship for me, and will be grieved to lose me. His visits have a better effect on me than quinine, they rejoice my heart and do not give me a pain in my stomach. He always says something droll to me which makes me laugh. He is witty, and expresses himself very happily. I would be an unnatural mother if I did not love him in the bottom of my heart; if you knew him well, you would see that there is no ambition or any malice in him. Ah, *Mein Gott*, he is but too good, he pardons all that they do against him, and only laughs at it. If he would show his teeth a little more to those bad relatives they would learn to fear him, and not to undertake horrible machinations against him." And again: "It is very true that it is better to be good than bad, but justice consists in punishing as well as rewarding, and it is certain that whoever does not make himself dreaded in France has soon cause for fear, because they despise him who does not intimidate them, that is why I wish my son were not as good as he is."

The next day, Madame wrote to Herr Von Harling: "I feel very sensible that I am approaching the limit of my seventy years, and if there comes to me a blow like that which struck me so rudely last year, I shall soon learn how things are going in the other world. My constitution remains good, and that is well shown in that I have endured all that has happened to me, but as the French proverb says, *Tant va la cruche a l'eau qu'a la fin elle se casse*, and that is what will happen to me at last. But my thoughts do not trouble me, because one knows very well, that one only comes into this world but to die, and I do not think that a long old age would be a very agreeable thing, one has too much to suffer, and when it comes to suffering, I am a great coward."

Her thoughts went back to the home of her childhood and she wrote again, to the Countess Louise: "There is not in the world better air than that of Heidelberg, and above all, that of the Château where my apartment is. Nothing better could be found. No one can comprehend more than I what you must feel at Heidelberg, I cannot dream of it without tears, but I cannot speak of this to-night, it makes me too sad and will keep me from sleeping."

On the 29th of September, 1722, Madame wrote to Herr Von Harling: "I do what my doctor orders so as not to be tormented but I wait the hand of Almighty God who will decide my case, I am entirely resigned to his will."

The young King was to be crowned at Rheims and Madame desired to attend the ceremony, the more especially as the family of the Duke of Lorraine would be present, and the occasion would give her the opportunity of seeing again her beloved daughter and her grandchildren. St. Simon said that, apart from Madame's apprehension with regard to her own health, she dreaded to leave her old friend and attendant the Meréchale de Clérambaut, who was now a very old lady. The Meréchale, who was credited with occult powers which were thought to enable her to foretell coming events, reassured her mistress and told her she need not hesitate to leave her as she would find her in good health on her return, and would herself outlive her. Madame finally decided to go.

Upon her return, she gave the following account of the excursion to the Countess Louise, written from Paris, November 5, 1722: " I came back yesterday in a sad state. During my journey I received five of your good letters. I thank you very sincerely because they gave me great pleasure. I did not reply because of my weakness and the continual turmoil where I have been. My time was all taken up by the ceremonies, by my children whom I had constantly about me, and by a crowd of distinguished people, princes, dukes, cardinals, archbishops and bishops, who came to see me. I do not believe that in the whole world one could imagine anything more magnificent than the coronation of the King. If God leaves me a little health I will give you a description of it. My daughter was much moved at seeing me, she had hardly believed in my illness, and imagined it was only a little fatigue, but when she saw me at Rheims, she was so much shocked that the tears came into her eyes, it made me feel sorry for her. Her children are good-looking, I believe the eldest will be a giant, he is as yet only fifteen and his height is extraordinary. The four others are neither large nor small, the younger, Charles, is extremely droll, he diverts himself with his sisters with many pleasantries, one might say of him, to use one of our father's expressions, 'his tongue will not rust in his mouth.' The prettiest of the three, in my opinion, is the second, as to the girls, the youngest is without doubt the prettiest, but the oldest has so pleasing an expression that one cannot call her ugly. I would like to talk longer with you, but I am too weak."

A week afterward, Madame promised to send the account of the coronation the day after the morrow, and said that she had been told something which gave her great joy, and that was that her son was about to reform his life, because he could not give so bad an example to the young King without incurring just reproaches. His mother hoped God might dispose him to keep these good resolutions and also give him every happiness. For herself, she had no concern as to what might be His will. On the 21st of November, she wrote as follows: "I become weaker hour by hour and suffer night and day, nothing helps me at all. I have great need that God should grant me patience. It will be a great favor to me if he will deliver me from my suffering. Do not afflict yourself, therefore, if you lose me, for it will be a great happiness for me."

A few days afterward Madame wrote that the Meréchale de Clérambaut was not well, and on the 29th of November she announced her death in the following words: "You will receive but a short letter from me to-day. I am more ill than I have ever been, and have not been able to close my eyes the whole night. Yesterday morning, we lost our poor Meréchale de Clérambaut. She did not have any illness, it was just as if life left her. This gives me a sincere sorrow, because she was a lady of great capacity and much merit. She was very well educated, although she did not display it. They say she has chosen the son of her eldest brother as her heir. It is not surprising to see a person of eighty-eight years pass away. It is always painful to lose a friend with whom one has passed fifty-one years, but I must stop, my dear Louise, I am too ill to say any more to-day. If you could see in what a sad state I am, you would comprehend how much I desire that this should be ended."

Nine days afterward, Madame died. To her son she said: "Why do you weep? Is it not necessary to die?" And to a lady of the Court who wished to kiss her hand, she said: "You may embrace me, for I am going to a country where all are equal."

Thus passed away one whose whole life had seemed but a tissue of contradictions and cross-purposes. Destiny placed her in a palace, while she might have been happier in a cottage. Her simple tastes would have been satisfied with an humble life, yet she was forced to endure the wearisome ceremonies of a court. Her good common-sense led her to estimate these things at their true value, yet such were the prejudices of her birth and education that she was filled with an undue reverence for rank and an almost superstitious veneration for its representatives. Although excessively bored by ceremony, she was ready to exact every iota of the respect due to her rank. Tender-hearted to a degree, she was relentless in her persecution of people who aspired to a higher station than that to which they were born. On one occasion her sharp rebuke of the assumption of a title which was not legitimate is said to have so mortified the young woman to whom it was addressed as to have caused her death. Madame related the incident in one of her letters without, apparently, having felt the slightest compunction for what she had done. It would have gratified her immensely to have known the high rank to which some of her descendants would afterward attain. But although her blood still flows in the veins of most of the royal personages of Europe, the representative of the House of Orleans is without a throne, and an exile from his country; while republicanism reigns in the palaces of his ancestors, and the ruins of Madame's beloved St. Cloud have been sold as so much rubbish. Madame was buried without pomp, being carried to St. Denis, followed by two carriages containing her son and some of her ladies, accompanied by a mounted escort of Swiss guards bearing torches.

The Duc d'Orleans outlived his mother but a year.

Lightning Source UK Ltd.
Milton Keynes UK
UKOW04f0506090517
300728UK00002B/168/P

9 781296 094591